*DEAL*BREAKER

The Definitive List of Dating Offenses

Dave Horwitz and Marisa Pinson
Illustrations by Tae Won Yu

RUNNING PRESS
PHILADELPHIA · LONDON

© 2010 by David Horwitz and Marisa Pinson
Illustrations © 2010 by Tae Won Yu

9 8 7 6 5 4 3 2 1

Digit on the right indicates the number of this printing

Library of Congress Control Number: 2010930716
ISBN 978-0-7624-4047-4

Cover and interior design by Jason Kayser
Edited by Jennifer Kasius
Typography: Akzidenz Grotesk and Century

Running Press Book Publishers
2300 Chestnut Street
Philadelphia, PA 19103-4371

Visit us on the web!
www.runningpress.com

For our parents, because if they were as picky
as we are, we'd have never been born.

Rough night, huh? Let's guess: you rushed over to your work friend Greg's art opening (who knew he was a painter as well as a file clerk?), only to discover that the gallery was a dimly lit room in a converted warehouse, and that he's not a painter but a "human paintbrush," which means that he flings his acrylic-soaked body at a blank canvas. Not exactly Norman Rockwell, but you went along with it because Greg's friend Mitch was there, and you sort of have a thing for him. Well, three paper cups of Two Buck Chuck later (way to go all out, Greg), Mitch is rambling on about his dream of owning a Hummer in between seismically enormous wine burps. If only he'd kept his mouth shut. Well, it's time to head back to your apartment, alone, and by choice this time.

Or perhaps you met your friends Barry and Curtis at a run-down little karaoke bar for a few pitchers of light beer and a laugh or two, when across the bar you spot the cutest girl in the room, Kim. In the oh-so flattering, dim red light of the bar, she's a knockout. You two hit it off because you have the same zodiac sign (Leos represent!), and because she's a vet tech and you've got a secret soft spot for sick kittens and three-legged dachshunds. Suddenly, your attention is diverted when Curtis belts out a surprisingly tuneful rendition of "Lovely Rita." He's got the crowd on their feet, all except for your beauty, who's covering her ears because she hates the Beatles—never "got" them. She thinks they sound like stupid cartoon music. *What?* Everything seems to go quiet for a moment. What kind of a person doesn't like the Beatles? The room starts to spin as you realize more and more imperfections in Kim's face until she might as well look like a potato with lipstick. You pay your tab, compliment Curtis on his hidden vocal talent, and get the hell out of there.

So, Mitch wasn't the right one for you, or even the right one for you to make out with in a cab. He might have a perfect five o'clock shadow, but his wine-stained purple teeth and gas guzzling dreams were enough to send you fleeing back to the safety of your room. And Kim's no prize either. I mean, seriously, hating the Beatles is a gateway to uncovering various other worldly horrors. If "Good Day Sunshine" doesn't make you smile, you've probably murdered a drifter at some point in your miserable life. At least you were able to spot these glaring turnoffs before things got really serious, or even before you did something you might regret involving hands, jobs, and gnawing your arm off so you can leave undetected in the morning.

That's just a small sampling of the vast collection of horror stories that lie ahead. If you've ever felt lost in a sea of dating disasters, nightmare hookups, and chance encounters that you'd rather not remember, welcome home. Give us your single, your casual hooking up, your totally jaded about relationships, yet still hitting up bars and clubs on a weekly basis. Give us your disastrous one-night stands and your blind dates that never made it past the breadsticks. We understand, and we're here to tell you: it's not your fault. And that's what this book is all about: Dealbreakers—anything that removes even the slightest hint of attraction you might have for a person. Let the record show, we're on your side. No matter how small the gripe, how minuscule the problem, we know that it can eat away at you until there's nothing left but your dissatisfaction with his wispy bangs, or her inability to chew with her mouth closed. We've heard your cries and your muffled screams, and we've seen the horror poorly hidden on your face.

We are the curators of a veritable museum of obnoxious human behavior, reprehensible character traits, and unacceptable physical attributes. This is our twenty-first century freak show, but instead of a roadside attraction in a dusty old town, these oddities are visible in plain sight: at your gym, winking at you from across the bar at Chili's, or popping up in your Match.com inbox. You don't have to travel to the county fair to spot someone you'd never want to share a bed (or even a beer) with.

We've compiled enough Dealbreakers to take you through the entire human population. We're here to represent the voice of a generation faced with an interesting contradiction: we are as obsessed with finding love as we are with avoiding it. This is a group who, unlike our parents, holds less value in our date's moral upbringing than what's on their iPod. Sure, it sounds shallow, but these cues are essential in finding Mr. or Ms. Right Now. Right here at this party. Jeez, lay off me I'm only twenty-eight and I'm not looking to settle down because I've got to think about my career and I've got shit to do like, um, I just started season 2 of *Battlestar Galactica* and who cares if my sister's twenty-two and just got married maybe that's what she wants right now but she's always had no ambition and that's fine if she just wants to pop out babies and call it a life—no I'm not drunk you're drunk!!

Shall we?

Chapter 1

The First Impression

The prospect of meeting someone you want to get in bed with at night is what makes you get out of bed in the morning.

Your mother was right, you never get a second chance to make a first impression. While she may have been referring to a job interview, the sentiment rings just as true when it comes to dating. Besides, what job is more important than the position of future apartment key holder? Trade your business casual attire and meticulously worded résumé for your lucky cardigan and charismatic small talk. In a loud, dimly lit bar, meaningful conversations are hard to come by, and in-depth evaluations of someone's personality are basically nonexistent. That's why we are limited to judge people on their most obvious means of representation: the first impression—the way they dress, style their hair, smell, and whatever small talk transcends the pumping base. All of this mixing and mingling can be met with indignation, indifference, desperation, or anything in between. However, all you need to know about dating is that regardless of how you feel about it, it is one of the most important parts of your early-mid-late-twenties. It lures you to spend too much time getting dressed and too much money on overpriced cocktails and have too many quarter-life crises. After all, the prospect of meeting someone you want to get in bed with at night is what makes you get out of bed in the morning!

So, here is your chance to shine, and lucky for you it couldn't be more convenient: Birthday Party for Your Best Friend at a Bar Near Your Apartment. You have all the right tools: clever anecdotes about your relationship with a mutual friend, a lighthearted take on politics, a charming story about the puppy you adopted (with accompanying photos on your cell phone). Your style is hip, yet casual, effortless, and approachable. Your friends are quick to describe you as a catch and eager to introduce you to equally eligible parties.

However, the star of this show is the biome of the dating climate: the Bar. Most patrons follow a similar ritual: scan the room, make small talk, check for text messages, go to the bathroom, order drink, and repeat. Men and women at this stage in life aren't particularly coy when it comes to preliminary mating rituals. It is perfectly acceptable to abandon some social decorum in exchange for the potential to get laid. Otherwise respectable men will hoot and holler at ladies who they find pleasing, while otherwise dignified women find themselves dancing on bar tops with reckless abandon. The crowd unites over their common goal, bopping in unison, buying rounds of drinks, throwing in a fist pump to the chorus of "Sweet Caroline."

You are forgiven for your indulgence in vices, knocking back whiskey after whiskey, cigarette after cigarette, nacho after nacho.You attack from humankind's most primitive state of mind with the force of natural selection lighting a fire under your ass. All this so you can hopefully, someday, maybe, like, *far* in the future, find someone to actually (gulp) settle down with.

Enter your prospect. You squeeze past the crowd for a better look, and as far as you can tell there's no immediate red flags—friendly, attractive, well-dressed, smiling. No dumb accessories as a desperate attempt to fit in with a peer group, no banal small talk, no bad smells. Suddenly you find yourself singing along to the Top Forty, swapping drinks, munching on maraschino cherries, giggling as you judge the room full of idiots. A hand finds its way to a knee, an arm around a shoulder. Could it be? Have you found the one person in this bar that you wouldn't be kicking yourself to be waking up next to? Maybe, but don't be celebrating too soon. They may seem to be miraculously devoid of any superficial Dealbreakers, but you've still got more investigating to do. There are plenty more deals to break and only an hour until last call. Get to work, boss.

Your Missed Connections

So, what you're telling me is that you felt an intense attraction to me when you saw me from across the supermarket as I was "reaching gracefully for a head of lettuce." Okay, well maybe I'm being naive here, but couldn't you have told me that in person? If I recall correctly, that particular shopping trip took me forty-five minutes (I guess that old saying is right, don't go to a grocery store hungry), meaning you had the better part of an hour to approach me face-to-face, or as you'd say, IRL? Maybe that would have been a little awkward, but less so than expecting to make a romantic connection with someone you were too scared to approach in the physical world. What did you think would happen: I would somehow read this (because you think I'm as crazy as you and I peruse Missed Connections looking to see if someone's watching me touch lettuce) and decide that it's time to fall in love with a Craigslist Troll? You don't need to Ask Jeeves, I'll tell you right now: it ain't gonna happen.

○ ○ ○   Missed Connections

Tan leather in checkout aisle 10 - m4w (Whole Foods/Third Street)

(Reply To This Post)

It was closing time and I was behind you -- you: tan skirt, tan jacket, dark hair to the middle of your back. By the time I was bagged up you were gone. Was that an engagement ring on your left hand or was I seeing things? Tell me what you were buying and I'll take care of everything else. And I mean *everything* else.

- Location: Whole Foods/Third Street

Your Nonprescription Glasses

At least these are aiding someone's vision: mine. I can see that you are a pretentious asshole.

Your Ironic Mustache

You're right, the funniest thing you ever did was grow a
shitty mustache. If you commit to this joke any longer you
won't be allowed to live within a thousand feet of an
elementary school.

You're a Creep

I'm getting an overall vibe here. It's not necessarily that you're dangerous, it's just that you would be someone that danger would follow. Think person of interest in a murder investigation. Maybe you're not the one who poisoned the drink, but you're the one who provided the poison, or gave a thorough and informative tutorial about how to make it. Does that make sense? Look, I can't help the way I feel, so please don't be angry with me or follow me to my car and make animal noises at me. Not that I'm saying that's something you do, just that it's something you're probably capable of. Like, you could do that in your sleep. Also, please don't kill me in my sleep.

You're a Self-Proclaimed "Bad Girl"

You know who was a bad girl? Amelia Earhart. She was the first woman to fly across the fucking Atlantic *and* Pacific oceans *by herself.* You know who else? Harriet Tubman. That lady was a motherfucking *spy* and risked her life to rescue a buttload of slaves. And Rosa Parks! She didn't give a *fuck* about segregation laws! What you're referring to is making out with other girls for free cocktails, getting in spitting fights outside of nightclubs, and having your rent paid by some old-ass divorced guy in exchange for sad handjobs. Grow some balls.

You're the Skankiest Girl at the Bar

Nice to meet you, Miss "Is My Pussy Showing?" However, after your bar-top gyrations, body shot administering, and a haphazard rendition of "I Love Rock and Roll," introductions feel superfluous. Why, you've been the center of attention all night! With an entire bar full of patrons as witness to your debauchery, a handshake feels far too formal. Yes, too formal in the way that wearing a bra was too formal, so you took it off under your tank top. It's for this reason I feel as if it would be unjust to keep you all to myself. A delicate flower like you is meant to be free, blowing in the evening breeze to enchant every presence she graces. Or, at least whatever presence is left over once last call is announced. May your voyages be safe, may your wisdom enlighten all you encounter, and may you always make it home with your underwear in your purse.

Your Idea of Dancing

Hey, pal. Can you get your erect penis away from my skirt? I'd like to leave this club with a mild buzz and a safe ride home, not an unplanned pregnancy.

You're Hitting on Everyone

Oh wow, it's my turn?? Finally, I get to meet the special dude
who wants to be all things to all people in this bar! To what do I
owe the pleasure? Let me guess, I'm standing here? You've
already whispered and/or yelled at eveyone else in this bar,
inanimate objects included, and you've made your way over to
me at long last. Okay, you've got twenty seconds. "Hi"? That's
your opener? Terrific, what else? I'm the "prettiest girl in here"?
Really? Because I think I just heard you say that to the blond
girl over there. And the brunette behind her. And that dude. And
that coat rack. Way to make a lady feel special, boss.

You're a Crazy Girl
(Nope, You're Just Loud)

Oh, hey. Mr. Blue Shirt? Are you talking to—oh I see, I have a blue shirt on. That's great, changing the lyrics to Mr. Blue Sky to Mr. Blue Shirt sounds wonderful, especially right in my ear. You think I'm a Cutey McCuterson? That's, um, flattering? Oh, I get it, you're the crazy one in your group of friends, right? I bet you're the one who organizes trips to see *The Rocky Horror Picture Show*, and I'm almost positive you're the go-to girl for planning a bachelorette party. Yep, you probably have penis-shaped cakes down to a sweet science. I've got a shiny quarter that says you were Sarah Palin for Halloween. I knew it. I just knew it.

You're a Cougar

Hey, Mrs. Richardson—okay, Candace, is Jeff home? We're
supposed to go to this party together. Oh, he already left? That's
too bad. I guess I'll just drive myself then…what's that? No, I
don't want a Mike's Hard Lemonade, I have to drive, and also
I'm seventeen. Why do you keep winking at me? Are
you okay? Is your skin permanently like that? Oh,
it's a spray tan. Cool. Well, I hope you have fun at
the club. No, I don't want to zip up your
minidress. Okay, okay. Here. Oh man, this
thing does not want to budge. No, I don't
think a butterfly tattoo would be sexy. Listen,
your aged wine and cheese analogies aren't lost
on me, but I'll pass. Good luck not appearing
outwardly sad tonight.

Your Facebook Page

Oh dear god no.

Your Facebook page is a veritable fire sale of turnoffs. Everything must go!

What. The. Fuck. I mean, I could have seen the warning signs, but you were just so charming. You really disarmed me, so I wasn't counting on your online presence boasting such a cornucopia of terrible. Seriously, this page is like an all-you-can-eat buffet of Suck.

P.S.: Favorite TV show: Autopsy??? There are no words.

○ ○ ○   Facebook

It's thirsty Thursday and I'm getting crunk!

About Me

Basic Info

Sex:	**Male**
Birthday:	**February 27, 1979**
Relationship Status:	**Single**
Interested In:	**Women**
Looking For:	**Dating**
	A Relationship
Hometown:	**Philadelphia, PA**
Political Views:	**American Idol**

Likes and Interests

Hobbies	Cosplay!
Music	Whatever's on the radio!
Recently Joined Groups	Thank God For Prop 8!
Favorite Quote	"Don't cry because it's over, smile because it happened"

"It's Complicated" and We Don't Want to Know about It

Some people are in relationships that contain a fair amount of gray area. They fight, they break up, they make up, they get back together, only to repeat the exact sequence a week later. They're confused, they're clouded by hormones and emotions, and of course, hormotions, which are hormonal emotions.

These couples argue loudly at gatherings, speak in muted, hushed tones to each other at dinner parties, get into screaming matches on the front porch, throw wine glasses at each other, and eventually end up boning in an upstairs bathroom. These relationships are anything but easy, far from normal, and fairly hard to succinctly explain.

Relationships like this are sprawling, unending, and often baffling, like a mobius strip. Those who are in them are often times not exceptionally happy, at least not all the time. They're frustrated and often unsatisfied, albeit between bouts of makeup sex-related elation.

However, temporary happiness aside, do these couples really want to broadcast that information to the world? We know it's ridiculous to even talk about Facebook like it's in any way a reflection of real life, but some people generally do try to represent their true selves online. Mostly, we've seen people use the "It's Complicated" relationship status as a joke. It's Complicated with their bffff(f), It's Complicated with their roommate, gay best friend, etc. We even know someone who went to the trouble of setting up a second account so his status read "It's Complicated With My Hands," and clicking on "My Hands" linked to a profile of his hands. That's... dedication?

For those looking to let people on the Internet know how great they are, there are many ways to display your accomplishments and impeccable taste on your Facebook profile. Look at me! I've read *Infinite Jest*, and it's one of my favorite books! I volunteer at four soup kitchens! I only like the *pre-Transatlanticism* Death Cab for Cutie albums! I can copy and paste poetry into the quote section! I work at Red Lobster! So, with all these other chances to brag, what's the need to describe the details of your weird relationship? We can't think of any reason someone would want to take the words "It's Complicated" to announce:

"Hey, I'm sort of seeing someone but I cheated on her and then begged her to take me back and she did but now we're not technically saying we're 'together' it's just this in-between phase because she says she can't really trust me anymore but maybe it'll work out if I can keep my dick in my pants long enough."

Ladies, where's the allure in intimating:

"So, I was dating this great guy and then I went to Europe to sort of find myself and backpack and do shrooms and one day I fell off my road bike in Rotterdam, and this really great guy came running out

of a coffee shop and he cleaned off my knee and bandaged it and took me inside and bought me a muffin and I was so grateful (and also high) that I ended up giving him a hummer in the backroom and now my boyfriend is all 'well if you love Werner so much maybe you should stay in Europe and now I'm all 'AHHH what if I should stay here?'"

Maybe it's a willingness to overshare with anyone and everyone who might Google you, but I'm pretty sure it's just their way of saying "yeah, I might not have a 'boyfriend' or 'girlfriend' *per se*, but at least I'm getting laid."

You're Not Mark Ruffalo

Look, we've tried everything, but you're
not Mark Ruffalo. You're a really great
guy, but you'll never be the star of such
films as *Zodiac* and *The Brothers Bloom*,
and you'll never be as mumbly and
handsome. I'm sorry, but I guess you can't
count on me. Please leave.

You Look Nothing Like Your Picture

"Oh, I'm sorry, this seat's taken. I'm meeting someone here. Wait,
Karen? Oh, my—well, Hey you. Ha! You're here. Yeaaaaaah. Sit
down, sure! No, I just, it's dark in here and I thought you
were...someone else. Must be time for an eye exam! Wow! Um,
so...did you have any trouble finding the place? Parking was a
nightmare for me and—okay, I'm sorry, I have to ask: Are you
really Karen? KGirl26? Grew up in Thousand Oaks? Did
modeling in Canada last summer? Huh, imagine that... No no, of
course I believe you, it's just, the pictures on
your profile make you look so
much more, human? No
wonder you listed 'Photoshop'
under hobbies..."

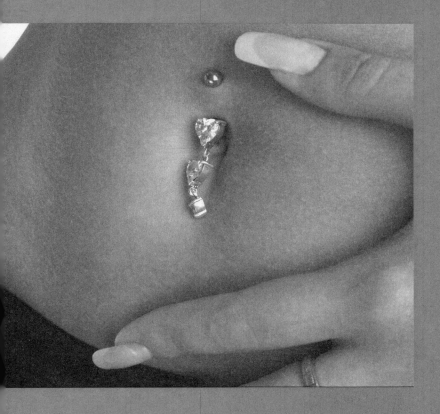

Your Belly Button Ring

There is a pile of cubic zirconia hanging from your waist. Get out of my car.

You're an American Apparel Model

Okay, so we've been dating for a while now and you have yet to put pants on. I'm sorry, but I can't introduce you to my family while you're wearing a see-through mesh bodysuit. I just don't think my grandmother would appreciate an up-close view of your vagina. Just a hunch I had. Ugh. This is really hard for me to say, but—I'm sorry, can you cover your nipples for *one* second? This is kind of important. I don't think this is working out, and—no, I don't know where you can get some more "fairy dust," whatever that means, but that's sort of the prob—it's really hard for me to have this conversation with you when you're writhing around on the floor like a sexy jellyfish. Use your bones like people do. Also, you're always rubbing your eyes and looking bewildered like you just woke up from a nightmare. Have you been sleeping on the floor again? Oh, this is pretty troubling, but you seem to have a habit of yelling "Dov!" while we're having sex and then bursting out laughing and *then* crying. You know that's not my name, right? And how many "corporate retreats" does your company take you on? You're always leaving for days on end, and you always wake up in dingy basements. Your "job" is starting to sound like you're just being routinely kidnapped every few days. Well, I guess that's it. I actually feel a lot better, thanks for finally listening. Babe? Sweetie? You okay?

Oh shit. Oh no! Wake up! Does anyone have any oversized sunglasses? Perhaps a Polaroid camera? Some sugar-free Red Bull, maybe? Get me a flash drive with Girl Talk on it, STAT! A life is hanging in the balance!

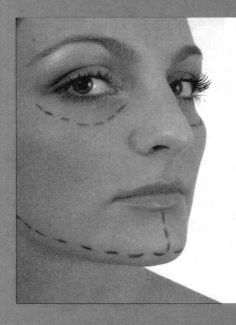

Your Unnecessary Plastic Surgery

I wish I could see past your Brazilian butt lift, lip injections, tattooed-on eyebrows, bolted-on breasts, cheek-implanted expressionless Botox face to get to know the real you. Oh never mind, the real you is an insecure idiot who spent $75,000 of her father's money to make herself look like a blow-up doll (which I might as well have bought for the price of your entrée). Here's a suggestion: next time you're going under the knife, upgrade to the brain transplant.

Your Slutty Halloween Costume

Um, a white tube top and a white miniskirt? That's your costume? That doesn't make you a "sexy angel," that just makes you sexy. Sunglasses and a bra doesn't make you a "hot cop," it just makes you a skank with weakened nighttime vision. And putting a sash over your underwear doesn't make you a beauty queen, it makes you a target for a sex crime. Please drape my jacket over your shoulders so you can be "Sexy Decreased Chance of Being Assaulted."

You're Too Hot

Would you please drape this tarp over your head when we go out in public? Ugh. At least wear this decorative face mask I made for you? Please, you're giving the entire universe an inferiority complex. I have no idea why you decided to go out with me in the first place, but if you think it's exciting for me to be dating an eleven out of ten, think again. I'm just waiting for the other shoe to drop. Is this a trick? Did a millionaire enlist you in a game called "humiliate the normal guy"? Did I win a contest? Was there a mistake at the Make-a-Wish Foundation? I'm not dying! I mean, you're even out of your own league! Seriously, I bet you wouldn't even have sex with you! Try it! I bet your body will reject your hand. You are a model! Not a fashion model, but a model of what every woman wishes *Fine!* Show your face! Oh no, people are looking…nothing to see here buddy, it's just a stunningly beautiful girl talking to a troll. Move it along.

Your "Picture Face."

Picture time! Okay girls, one… two…three… say "I-look-sexy-
but-also-like-a-funny-girl-you-know-a-girl-who-is-okay-with-
looking-a-little-silly-in-a-picture-but-also-supercute-and-festive-
and-having-a-lot-of-fun-being-single-in-case-my-ex-boyfriend-
sees-this-on-Facebook!"

Your Cucumber Melon Body Spray

Look, I'm sure you were an attractive thirteen-year-old, but if I wanted to feel like I was in the eighth grade again, I'd go hang out at a junior high school. But then I'd probably get arrested, so, you know, take a shower and call me when you smell like a grown-up.

Your Marilyn Monroe Piercing

Oh sure...that metal in your face makes you look exactly like
that famous dead lady. Don't tell anyone we fucked.

Your Excessive Body Hair

A disposable razor costs $1.07. Your argument is invalid.

Your Dumb Hat

With this crown, I dub thee King Douche.

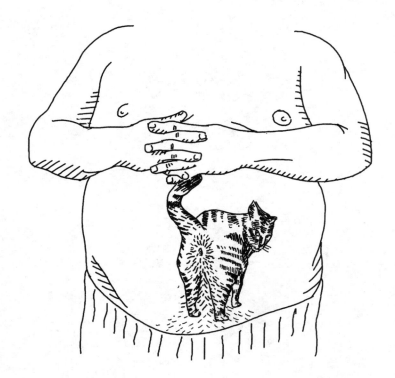

Your "Funny" Tattoo

If your body is a joke, and your tattoo is the punchline, I guess the setup would be, "a girl walks into a bar and makes a really bad decision."

Your Hygiene

Did you come here straight from work? The gym? The airport? Camping? Collecting garbage? Fixing a tractor? Working on a shrimp boat? Being stranded on an island? Oh... from home? Is your hot water broken? Were you out of deodorant? Did your roommate use the last of the body wash? Did thieves steal your toothbrush? I see. So, you're an environmentalist? A hippie? European? Nope? Just dirty? Well, it looks like we're done here.

You Wear Too Much Makeup

Oh, wow. Is the circus in town? I think they're one clown short. Too easy, you say? Well, so are you with all that paint on your head.

Your Velcro Sandals

Hey! You showed up! Well, I hope you like barbecue because there's plenty of—hang on. What's going on with your lower body situation? Khaki's with weirdo hippie sandals? Did your left brain and right brain wage a war on your bottom half and this was their compromise? Make up your mind, weirdo, is it business or pleasure? It's great that you made the effort to roll out of bed and throw on a clean shirt, but at least slap some hush puppies on those barking dogs! If the embarrassment doesn't kill you, the fungal infection will. And what if you step in a puddle? Ugh, your feet are giving me a panic attack. Show me a man in his mid-twenties who is in such a hurry to go out and meet ladies that he has no time for socks or laces, and I will show you a man who will go a very long time without touching a boob.

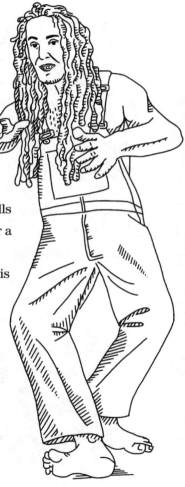

Your White Dreads

The mere smell of your patchouli oil fills me with dread. I've put up with this for a dreadfully long time, and now I am starting to dread seeing you. Your hair is dreadful. Do you see where I'm going with this? Of course you don't.

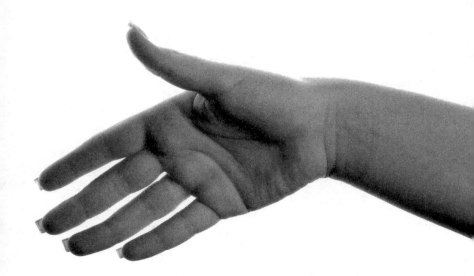

Your Weak Handshake

If I wanted dead fish, I'd go out for sushi.

With someone else.

Your Obviously Fake Tits

There's a catastrophe in Cashmere City. Trouble's a-brewin' in
Tank Top Town. Havoc has been unleashed in Halter Top
Harbor. An atrocity—ugh, whatever. Your tits are a mess.

Everything About You

Nope. Sorry. Not gonna happen. Back away slowly. I'm
restraining myself from being mean. Temptation is strong in me.
So. Easy. To. Say. Something. Mean. Must. Be. Polite. Smile,
nod, and walk away. Oh my god you're still here. Please make
this easy on both of us. Well, mostly me. Make it easy on me
and leave me alone so I don't have to experience any more
guilt, awkwardness, or embarrassment.

You're a Pickup Artist

So, your name is Laser Vision? Really? Is that your given name, or is that a really great way to start a conversation? Do I want to see a card trick? Now you're just answering a question with a question. Why do you want to know if I believe in the power of hypnotic suggestion. Oh. Wait a minute. I know what's going on. Look, man, I refuse to be just a feather in your pirate hat. You're as obvious and easy to read as the words on your scrolling LED belt buckle: you're a pickup artist! You've paid thousands of dollars learning how to trick women into sleeping with you, all with the precision of a Dungeons & Dragons enthusiast. I'm going to go talk to my normal friends now. You know, the ones who don't show up to bars wearing boa constrictors around their necks.

Your Style

Okay, I didn't even think I cared about this kind of thing until I saw you, but you are fucking magical! I mean, does your closet lead to Narnia, and does a fucking centaur dress you in the morning? You've struck some kind of impossible balance between not looking like you're trying too hard, but still looking like you just hopped off a runway in Milan. Milan? Fashion stuff happens there, right? Oh, fuck, who am I kidding? I don't know anything about fashion, and I certainly didn't think about it until I saw you. And now that I've seen you, I never want to not see you. Is there a way to do that without doing some kind of permanant damage to my eyes? If so, I want in.

You're Jeff Goldblum

He stands in my kitchen, his muscular frame silhouetted by the light of the open refrigerator. The days of making love have left me exhausted—I fight the urge to close my eyes by trying to recognize the tune he's been singing. It's a meandering melody, but it sounds familiar...as familiar as his breath on my cheek or the sound of his laugh buried in the pillows. He sits on the bed beside me, brushing my hair from my forehead. The song quiets until it becomes a whisper. And then, like that—he is gone. All that is left is a note:

"All good things must come to an end"

—*A T. Rex, on dinosaurs*

Chapter 2

The First Date

. . . the culmination of days, maybe even weeks of text, phone, and online flirting . . .

This is it. This is thunderdome. The time and place for money to be put where one's mouth is. You wanted a date, you got one! So now it's time to make it happen. This is the culmination of days, maybe even weeks of text, phone, and online flirting, not to mention the strategic planning leading up to it ("how soon is too soon to Facebook?" among other psychotic thoughts). You've laid the foundation, and decided it was worth it to see this thing through to an actual sit-down, talk-about-your-life, order-wine-instead-of-beer, *date*. Be forewarned, though: the first date is a veritable gauntlet of potential Dealbreakers, an obstacle course of avoidable weirdos. But you have to weather the storm if you're going to make it through the night. So batten down the hatches and swab the mixed metaphors, because we're off to the races.

You've done your homework leading up to this point, and for that, you should be commended. You headed straight from the bar, or party, or post office (what a weird place to be hit on) armed with a phone number and a full name, and you've taken it straight to Google. Thank you, privacy-compromising, all-encompassing, no-stone-unturned search engine! You'll gladly trade your social security number and Ebay purchase history for a few choice photos of your intended date! And why not? It's important to be as thorough as possible from the outset.

The Internet is a treasure trove of information about strangers you just met! In fact, if you sought this information out in the waking world, you'd be a stalker! But, no matter! You're not in the waking world, you're on the Internet, and the Internet told you that your date won a Swim Meet in 1997! Hey, that's interesting! By now, you've read their blog, you've scoured 450 of their Facebook pictures, and you've found microfiche of their hometown newspaper. They seem normal enough and even attractive. Now get out there and meet up with them!

The pressure's on, but you're keeping a cool head. You've got your meticulously-planned-but-not-overly-dressy clothing decision, your subtle but noticeable scent, your understated but noteworthy body grooming (nice trim!), and now you're ready to impress! The question is: what's up with your date? What the hell is going on? Wait, calm down, you. You're better than this. You're not so judgmental, right? You're open-minded! You picked an Ethiopian restaurant for this date, remember? You're eating with your hands! And yet, your date won't stop yapping, and not about anything interesting either. Oh no. STOP IT! This date isn't ruined! Look past it! Smile! Change the subject! You're being challenged, and suddenly this date becomes a game show. You can either choose to ignore all of the things that are laid out on the table for you to notice and dislike, OR you could look past all of that and choose door number two: a postdate drink and maybe a sloppy car makeout session? And you without the shouted suggestions of a studio audience. I guess you're just going to have to trust your gut on this one. Your drunk, slightly horny gut...

You're Late

"I run on my own clock" is neither cute nor an acceptable excuse when you show up more than an hour and a half late. Saying you're going to "pop in the shower and be right over" is also bullshit, although it is fascinating that you have a wormhole in your bathroom.

You Sit on the Same Side of the Booth

Hey! No I haven't been waiting long, I just ordered a Coke. Um... is someone else going to be joining us? No? So I just move over and you slide in right up next to me? And we both just stare straight forward across the table at those empty chairs? And I am crammed against this wall like I have a window seat on an airplane? And you need shoulder to shoulder contact throughout this whole meal? And I have to be conscious of not jabbing you with my elbow while I eat my BLT? And depend on you to hand me the ketchup because it's out of my reach? And surrender my freedom to leave without asking you to get up first? I'm sorry, can you please scooch out so I can go to the bathroom? I am going to be sick.

Your Choice Of Location

Hey, you're a pretty cool girl. It's not every day that a guy gets picked up by his date and whisked to a mystery location. I have to admit, I'm impressed. Oh, we're here. What the—The Holocaust Museum? You're joking right? There's gotta be a roller rink or a carnival next door—huh. No, I'm not interested in growing closer by exploring a horrific historical tragedy that exterminated millions of people. You got a backup plan? Perhaps a walking tour of a slaughterhouse, or maybe a garbage pile that we can roll around in? That's our next date? Perfect.

You're a Liar

Something is fishy here... well for starters, your "homeboy" Ashton Kutcher is "mysteriously not answering his cell phone" to let us into this club. And your "tricked out Maserati" is "in the shop" so we drove here in my Passat. And your "loft overlooking downtown" is "being fumigated," so I had to pick you up in front of a deli. Let me guess: you "left your wallet at home" so you don't have cash for the valet? Well, I'd love to stay, but my BFF Madonna got attacked by a space dragon, and I have to take her to the jellybean hospital. What, you don't believe me?

Your Cologne

Thanks a lot, buddy. Now I'll never be able to go to a hookah bar, car show, or discotheque without being reminded of you. I'm sure you'll find someone else who appreciates the smell of shoe leather and bottle service.

You Won't Put Down Your Cell Phone

So, texting your besties, updating your Facebook status, checking tomorrow's weather forecast, looking up the release date of *Babe 2: Pig in the City*, reading your daily horoscope, and Googling the calories in an egg roll is more interesting than this living, breathing, sentient being sitting across from you? I hope you and that two-inch-by-four-inch glowing screen are having a good time because this just became a table for one. You know, because I'm leaving? Standing up? Pushing in my chair now. Hello? Nothing? Never mind, I'll text you about this later.

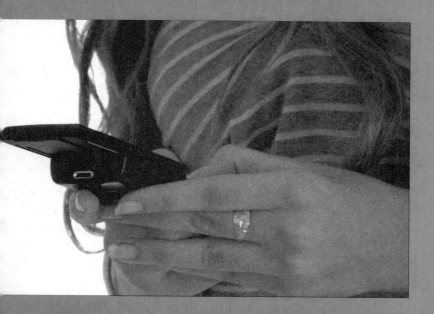

You Order for Me

I've never been here before, this menu looks great! Hmm...
pastas, salads, breadsticks, soups...I'm sorry, I'm going to need
at least a few minutes to decide. What's that? It's taken care of?
But-but-but. Ordering for ourselves is one of our basic
freedoms! This is a step backward in women's rights! This is
what our ancestors fought for! I might have slept through most
of Gender Studies, but I do know this: that Gloria Steinem lady
would *not* approve.

You Won't Stop Talking About Your Ex

Wait, I think you've told me this story before. It ends with your ex saving a baby from a burning building. No? Oh, it's the one about how he took you to a private island owned by his billionaire father? Or maybe it's about how the only reason you two broke up was because he had to go on a humanitarian mission in Africa! You know what, if you like him so much, why don't you go live with him in his sweaty, mosquito-infested tent? Oh, I get it. *That's* how this story ends.

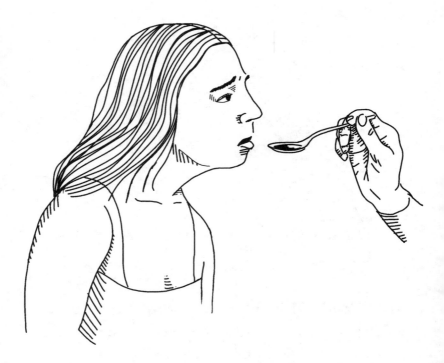

You Keep Trying to Feed Me

Yes, I have heard that chocolate is an aphrodisiac. You know what isn't? You shoveling cake into my face. I am not a baby, and you are not Mickey Rourke in *9½ Weeks*.

Your Lack of Manners

I don't need to be greeted with a bouquet of roses and a box of chocolates, but perhaps there is something to be said for opening a door, saying please and thank you, and not dunking your buffalo wing fingers into my milkshake to fish out the maraschino cherry. Or excusing yourself from the table to "have a meeting with Mayor McTurd." No, I'm not being sexist, I'm calling a spade a spade, here. Oh, and by the by, wearing shoes to a date isn't necessary, but it is customary.

You Talk Through Movies

Um, yeah, that's the good guy. Because he—yeah, I know he's wearing the same uniform as the bad guy. He's undercover trying to infiltrate-expose, *shhh!* Okay, look, Matt Damon is the one on the right, and Paul Giamatti—the sort of shlubby looking—I don't know why he's in this movie, but he is, *shhh*, that's Jessica Biel, not Alba, no—I don't know if that's her real hair color. Yeah, sure she's pretty. No, not prettier than you. Okay, you talked through the big plot twist, and now I'm actually lost. I'm going to go get some popcorn… at my house. How's that for a twist?

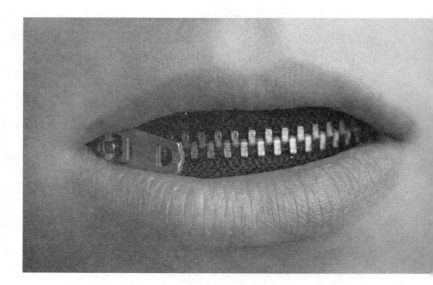

You're a Narcissist

Maybe you'll tear yourself away from your reflection in the window behind me long enough to notice I've left. Save the $15 and revert back your usual Saturday night plans of taking camera phone pictures of your abs and jerking off in the mirror.

You're Rude to Waiters

While you're busy snapping your fingers to get a
refill on breadsticks, sending your soup back
because you oversalted it, and complaining to
the manager about the price of the cheesecake,
I'll be getting my food to go. Here's a tip: 15
percent is standard, 20 percent is exceptional,
and 0 percent is the likelihood of a second date.

You're a Gross Eater

It sounds like you're doing sound effects for *Beethoven's 3rd*. You've used up all the napkins by mopping up the sauce that dripped down your wrists, your neck, and in your eyebrows. How did you get sauce in your eyebrows? You rival an eight-month-old in your food to face-to-table ratio. It's not adorable. It's disgusting. Bits of your meal are hurling themselves across the table threatening to land on my face. You'd be better off forgoing silverware all together and smacking the plate directly at your head. I'm almost losing my appetite for these unlimited breadsticks. *Almost.*

Your Joke T-Shirts

Brett,

First of all, sorry I left early last night. Thanks for taking me to Dave & Buster's, who knew butterfly shrimp and skee ball went together so well? Unfortunately, I don't think this is going to work. I'll leave your Smash Mouth CD in your mailbox.

Best,

Jennifer

P.S. Vote For Pedro? Seriously? That movie is from 2004! Not even Pedro would wear that! Except maybe on laundry day. *Maybe.*

You Won't Take Out Your Bluetooth

I'm fine, thanks. That's a strange thing to ask in the middle of a date. Later tonight? Hmm, I hadn't planned anything after dinner, although we could go see a movie or something. That could be fun, actually. I haven't seen the new—wait, what? I don't want to go golfing tomorrow, I just told you I work during the day. Oh my god. You're talking to your friend Bryce. In the middle of a date. And you needed your hands free so you could eat steak and ignore me more comfortably. I should have recognized the blinking blue light emitting from your head as a douche signal.

We Work Together

Office romance, how I love thee! Let me count the ways! The way your hair shimmers under the fluorescent lights. The way you laughed when I made you a crown out of paperclips and dubbed you "The King of the Supply Closet." The way you saved every Dilbert cartoon I ever left in your cubicle. The way our hands touched at the copier one fateful Monday. The way we decided we weren't ashamed of our mutual flirtation and decided to give it an official try after that drunken holiday party makeout. The way we sat across from each other at Applebee's sharing an appetizer sampler. The way we have nothing in common beyond a shared hatred for office memos and our bosses pantsuits. The way you awkwardly tried to make me laugh with jokes that are staler than breakroom danish. The way that in this new, nonfluorescent light, you're nothing more than a schlubby guy in a stained dress shirt with a mouthful of jalapeño poppers. The way that I'll be taking to get to the bathroom until one of us is either fired or promoted to a different floor? The long way.

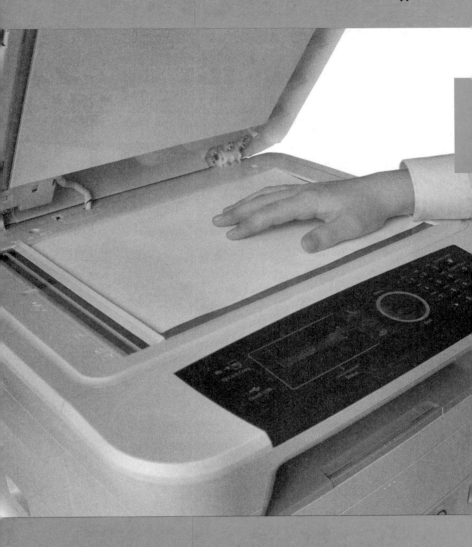

You're Trying to Get Me Drunk

Cool, quarter shot night! Awesome, haha! I'm good with a beer for now thanks. Yeah, just a beer. It's cool that the beer and whiskey shot special is only $3, but I'm not really interested in puking in my lap. What? No, I'm not a lightweight, I can handle my liquor pretty damn well, thank you very much. A challenge, you say? Why what an enticing proposal! So, basically, if I win, I get the honor of being crowned "awesome drinker," bestowed to me by a first date, and if I lose, I get to wind up propped up in the passenger seat of your, don't tell me, 1998 Corolla, while you attempt a little light groping before the main course, a night of passion that not even an elephant could remember. Next time, try having a personality. You'll find it to be a more intoxicating social lubricant than any bottom-shelf rubbbing alcohol.

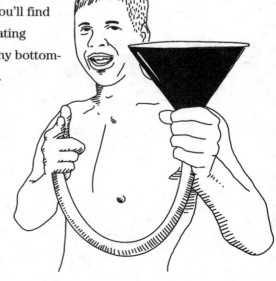

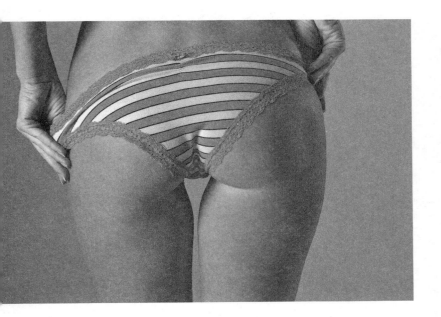

You Call Women's Underwear "Panties"

I'm assuming the desired effect was not to make me throw up in my mouth, so I'm gonna have to call this one a loss. It's that simple: if you can't mention them without disgusting me, you're probably not going to see them.

You're Boring

Ughhhhhh. I've been talking for twenty straight minutes. You're just nodding your head yes and half laughing at appropriate times. I'm filling silent gaps with stories I haven't dusted off in years! Help me out! Don't make me do all the conversational heavy lifting! Tell me something. *Anything!* Lie to me! Tell me you saw a dragon once! I don't give a shit, as long as it's interesting. Don't tell me about your great parking spot at the post office, because if that's the best you can do, I will take you to the blandest restaurant I can find, throw your Bloomin' Onion on the floor, and stick you with the bill. Don't think I won't.

You Don't Like Pizza

WHAT KIND OF A PERSON WOULD

I MEAN HONESTLY.

I JUST.

WHAT? WHAT THE FUCK. SHIT. I MEAN HOLY SHIT. SHIT SHIT SHIT SHIT SHIT. I HATE THIS. I HATE WHAT THIS IS. IS THIS EVEN HAPPENING? PIZZA? YOU DONT LIKE IT? WHAT ELSE DON'T YOU LIKE? BREATHING? JOY? SUNSHINE? I AM LEAVING AND I'M TAKING YOUR STUFF. THAT'S RIGHT, I'M TAKING ALL OF YOUR THINGS BECAUSE YOU DON'T DESERVE THEM! CALL ME WHEN YOU'RE READY TO JOIN THE HUMAN RACE.

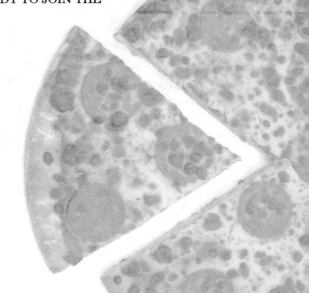

You're Saving Yourself for Marriage

Yeah, sure, sex is sacred and your body is a temple and blah blah blah. It's a lucky lady who finally earns the privilege of having terrible, inexperienced sex with you. Thank goodness you are redeemed by your "winning personality" and your "love of blow jobs."

You're "Not Really a Puppy Person"

Okay, let's be logical here. There's gotta be an acceptable reason why you don't like something as joyful and adorable as a puppy. You probably just had a traumatic experience with one as a child, right? Maybe a dog bit your face or something? No? Well, my other theory is that you're a space alien with thick black oil coursing through your veins and a heart made of garbage.

Do Dogs Have Dogbreakers?
A Special DEALBREAKER Exposé

Recently, Dealbreaker had the opportunity to sit down with our friend's dog, Freddy Mercury. In this exclusive interview, we learn all about canine dating and mating rituals. The results may surprise you.

Dealbreaker sets a tape recorder and a dog biscuit on the table. Freddy stops licking his dick and looks up.

Dealbreaker: Freddy, thanks for agreeing to this interview. What is your current relationship status?

Freddy: Yikes. If only Dogbook had an "It's Complicated" option, "nawmsayin"? Let's just say I'm trying to get out of the friend zone and into the (rear) end zone. Pun definitely intended.

Dealbreaker: You want to smell a girl's butt? Is that what you're—

Freddy: Look man, I mean if you hang out with a girl, show her a stick you're playing with, chase a few flies around, run away from a Rottweiler together, that's something, right? I mean, you guys had something!

Dealbreaker: Um. I woudn't know, man. I'm not a dog.

Freddy: I know, we can't all be perfect. (*laughs, lights a cigarette*)

Dealbreaker: You can't smoke in here.

Freddy: You see how cute I am? No one's gonna say shit, bro.

Dealbreaker: Okay, so, do you have any turnoffs? Any... Dealbreakers?

Freddy: What the fuck is a Dealbreaker?

Dealbreaker: It's something someone does to instantly turn you off to them.

Freddy: Turn… off?

Dealbreaker: Yeah. Something that grosses you out.

Freddy: Listen, guys. I eat poop, okay? Seems a little unfair to have a Dealbreaker about someone else, right? That's like the ultimate gross thing. Anyway, I'm not picky. I'm happier that way. Thanks for the biscuit. Later.

And with that, Freddy immediately became terrified of his reflection in the glass coffee table and ran away.

You're Cheap

When you're done squeezing a side order of lemons into a glass of water and filling it with packets of sugar, or as I call it, Sad Lemonade, can you hand me my purse? And go ahead and take out the saltine crackers, peppermint candy, tea bags, and silverware. Leave the water bottle you filled with vodka. I'll need that for the walk home.

You're a Bad Kisser

Kissing is like an entry-level position at the company known as My Pants. If you want to move up in the company, or, down in my pants, as it were, you need to apply yourself. This, of course, is an overly articulate way of saying, "hey, gross person, if you keep ramming your tongue down my throat like a disgusting monster, I'm going to suffocate and die."

You Put Something In My Drink

Hey there, slick, what's going on with my vodka soda? I turn my back for five seconds and now it looks like a sea monkey habitat. Let's not dance around the issue, dude: you're trying to drug me and take me to your creepy dungeon/parents' basement, right? Wow. If I knew I was eating dinner with a sex criminal, I wouldn't have bothered wearing makeup and a nice dress. And I wouldn't have showered. And told my friends. Or shown up at all. Actually, I'm a cop and this is a sting operation. Not really, I just wanted to see if you'd piss yourself. Annnnnd, jackpot.

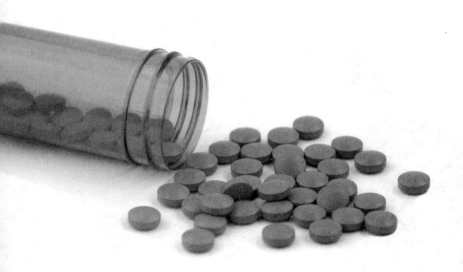

How To Make A Long Island Lowered Standard

You'll Need

1 King Size Commemorative Chili's Drink Tumbler (shaped like a football helmet)

1 oz Peach Schnapps

1 oz Triple Sec

1 oz Sweet 'n' Sour Mix

1 oz Green Apple Pucker

2 Drops Raspberry Fanta

36 oz Grain Alcohol

1 bag of Watermelon Jolly Ranchers

4 Pixy Stix (assorted colors)

1 PCP-Soaked Cigarette (or sherm as it's known on the street)

1 baggie of heroin

3 Unfulfilled Dreams

24 crushed-up Grape-Flavored Chewable Aspirin (to take the edge off)

A Smattering of Tears (to taste, you don't want it to be too sad)

1 set of Tongs

1 Gas Mask

1 small Pitchfork (note symbolism)

Directions

► Combine (while wearing the gas mask) all ingredients in Chili's Drink Tumbler. Stir with pitchfork until mixture has become a viscous goop, or "Slime."

► Using tongs, place under your date's nose and waft.

► Wait.

► DEALBREAKER is in no way responsible for what happens next.

► Please note: having a personality is a cheaper, less complicated, and legal way to achieve the same outcome.

► Enjoy!

You Drive a Hummer.

12 MPG City, 17 MPG Highway, 0 chance of you
seeing my boobs.

What's in this dude's glove box?

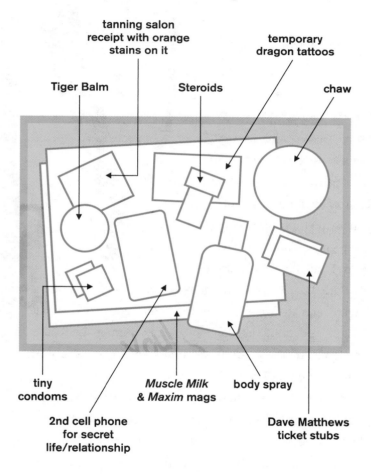

tanning salon
receipt with orange
stains on it

temporary
dragon tattoos

Tiger Balm

Steroids

chaw

tiny
condoms

Muscle Milk
& *Maxim* mags

body spray

2nd cell phone
for secret
life/relationship

Dave Matthews
ticket stubs

Your Sex Dungeon

Wow! This is going so well! You were so forward to invite me back to your place, but I think I'm totally into it! I mean, I don't usually do this, but whatever, you seem great. Cool, you have a house! Wow, I only have an apartment and—

oh. Sure, I'll take a tour of the basement. I mean, I'd rather see the upstairs but we can get to that later, right? Huh. Man it's dark in here, huh? Just some blacklight fixtures. Lots of leather, a wall of... are those paddles? Umm, look, I know that during dinner I said that I was adventurous, but I was sort of talking about spontaneous road trips and ethnic cuisine. No offense to your lifestyle choices, but I'm going to pass on the ball gag and chains. At least we can both agree that Nine Inch Nails made some really amazing music right? Ha! Anyway... please let me live. I've got some great stuff DVR'd at home.

You're Too Drunk

Wow, meeting for a drink is starting to seem like a questionable first date choice. I'm getting pretty hungry, and I kind of wish we'd have gone to a restaurant instead of the dive near your apartment. All your compliments are totally flattering, albeit a tad aggressive. Pulling at my arm, begging me to dance, and yelling in my ear, all the while reeking of a bar mat, is not exactly how I'd describe an ideal date companion. While you're knocking back your fifth margarita, I'll be closing the tab on my one beer. If you want to reach me, my number's in your phone. And your phone is in the men's room toilet. You'll probably figure that out in the morning.

You Misread the Vibe

This has been a terrible date. I'm sorry, I'm just being blunt. I see no future for the two of us, whether that be just as friends, casual dating, long-term romance, or anything in between. You and I have nothing in common, and even if we did, you are a repulsive human being. You didn't laugh at any of my jokes, you smell horrible, and you spent half the time on your phone. I see no reason to even continue this conversation, let alone this date. Good night. What? No you can't come upstairs! Are you fucking serious? Wait, did you really think this date was anything but a spectacular, unmitigated disaster? Personally, I'm shocked. I mean, you spit food on my sweater twenty minutes ago! I freaked out because I know that stain's never coming out. You will *never* see the inside of my apartment. I don't care that you make a "mean Manhattan," I literally *never* want to see you again. UGH, get off me! If ever a date called for a good-night macing instead of a good-night kiss, it's this one.

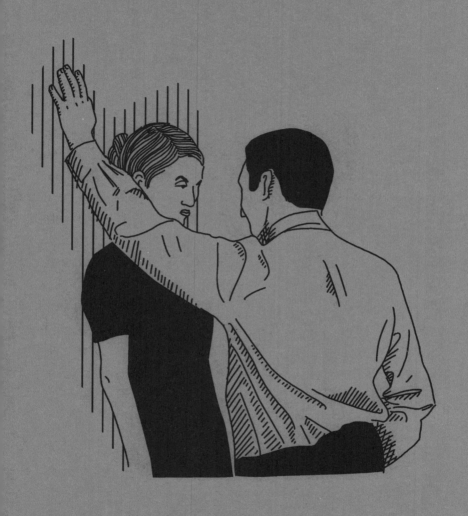

You're Bad at Sex

How can a reasonably good kisser miss the mark so far as soon as we become horizontal? You're clawing at my breasts like you're climbing a gorge! The sounds you are uttering sound like you're struggling to breathe! Oh my god, now what are you doing? That action can only be described as gnawing, and it has no place in the bedroom! The rhythm is off, the lighting is terrible, the whole performance is a fiasco. I'm afraid I'm gonna have to tap out of this match, coach. At least I can bow out gracefully before you finish—never mind.

You Laugh at My Jokes

Dating someone who doesn't think I'm funny is like spending every night being booed and heckled at some hellish comedy club you can't escape from. I thank God for the fact that not only are you not pelting me with rotten produce every time I try to make a witty observation at dinner, you're actually *laughing*! You're like the world's kindest, most supportive, and best-looking open mike audience . . . that I get to have sex with.

You're the Right Kind of Nice

Look, there are a few different kinds of nice. There's boring nice, which describes the kind of person you'd tolerate as a coworker or a tangential member of your group of friends. They're sweet, helpful, harmless, and maybe a little boring. Then there's the aggressive kind of nice: the kind of nice that's in your face, eerily desperate, and says "I'll do anything with a smile even if I don't really want to." That kind of nice leaves me with a bad taste in my mouth, sort of like drinking diet soda. Then there's you. You just seem... *nice*. And sure, there are lot of of other great things about you, but sometimes nice can be refreshing when I spend all my time dealing with weirdos and creeps and bitchy assholes. Sometimes a little nice goes a long way.

Chapter 3

The Morning After

Whatever act they put on the night before, no matter how cool they played it, this is where their true colors will really shine through.

Morning, Sunshine! Sheesh, how many drinks did you have last night? Didn't plan on spending the night but it just sort of happened, huh? No judgment from this corner, we've all been there. Nonetheless, congratulations on making it this far.

There is no moment more indicative of the direction of a relationship than the morning after. Both parties are vulnerable, hungover, in need of a hose-down, and now have to pay dues for the (possible) mistakes made eight hours prior. What might have seemed like a good idea (or good enough idea) in a dark bedroom with a well-constructed iTunes mix can be revealed by the morning light as another step in your descent to rock bottom. Who is this person snoring beside you? Sure, you had a good time: the drinks were flowing, the entrees were shared, small talk quickly gave way to an actual, engaging conversation. However, don't start celebrating too soon—all of those positive qualities can be negated quicker than the time it took to respond to the offer to come upstairs.

You have the upperhand when in someone's apartment. It is here that you can observe physical representations of their brain, each one more revealing than the next. And at your first moment of discontent, you have the freedom to haul ass out of there without so much as a kiss good-bye. This is it. The naked truth. Whatever act they put on the night before, no matter how cool they played it, this is where their true colors will really shine through.

Make yourself at home, survey your surroundings. You have the break of dawn to illuminate this personality buffet that is laid out before you. These walls are talking and they are speaking volumes of last night's conquest: their taste, their interests, how they keep their home, even the way they approach the situation you both are in. Mismatched IKEA furniture or vintage thrift-store finds? A refrigerator containing a bounty of organic produce and homemade leftovers or two beers and questionable take-out? There is even the ground zero of your potential calamity: a high thread-count duvet or a stripped mattress on the floor? Splash some water on your face, pour yourself a glass of orange juice (if there is any), pull up a chair beside their CD rack, scope the photos lining the hallway, and get to work, Sherlock. Take an inventory of this current situation and don't forget to turn those prescription bottles back to the angle you found them. Now choose one of two paths: throw on your coat and call a cab, never to be heard from again, or start making plans for brunch. This choice is a crucial one, and it's all yours.

Your Sleeping Arrangement

Nice, dude. Way to transform an otherwise pleasant hookup into a weird, grungy, and downright miserable experience for me. You couldn't step your game up even a *little*, could you? I mean, you seemed to know how to dress yourself and you even paid for dinner, so I don't think it's unreasonable to expect a bed frame, or sheets, or a *bed*. What is this thing? Is this just a pile of blankets on an exercise mat? Oh. It's just a pile of blankets. *Of course* you don't own an exercise mat.

Your Morning Breath

Top o' the Morning to You, Stink Face! According to popular folklore, vampires turn to dust in the morning light. According to my nose, however, your mouth turns into a septic tank. That information would have been valuable eight hours ago when your soon to be garbage barge was wreaking a unique brand of havoc on my body. May the future bring you mints, gum, mouthwash, and my sincere hope that we never come face-to-face, or mouth to nose, ever again.

You Don't Want Breakfast

Wakey wakey, eggs and bakey! I hope you're ready to experience the ultimate omelet, as well as the best homemade hash browns you've ever tasted. See, what I do is add a little cumin and rosemary and—huh? You're joking, right? Please tell me you're joking. You'll just have coffee? *Just coffee?* You're "not into breakfast"? Excuse me, but the only things that make getting up before noon even remotely worthwhile are bacon, eggs, toast, pancakes, waffles—oh shit, my mouth's watering. I'm outta here. I've got to get to IHOP. I don't think I've been this disappointed since... *last night! In your face, Egg Hater!*

Your Dreamcatcher

I thought the folklore of a dreamcatcher was to keep nightmares away, not present them in my waking reality.

You Live with Your Parents

If "Shhhh, my dad's a really light sleeper" is your idea of dirty talk, then I'm going home. Also, I'm gonna need a little help getting down from the top bunk.

You Bought a Zune

Hey, you're awake. I'm sorry, I just don't know how to do this. Look, last night was fun, and I really thought I could get past this, but I was wrong. You bought a Zune. A Microsoft Zune! There's nothing you can say to redeem yourself. I don't care that you can listen to the radio on it. I don't care that you can "Zap" music to your friends. All I care about is being seen in public with someone who needs to cart their music around on a hunk of plastic the size of a toliet seat. Size doesn't always matter, baby.

Your Devil Sticks

1993 called, they want their—aw fuck it, I'm leaving.

Your Empty Kitchen

I can totally understand being nineteen and living in your first apartment. Of course you're not accustomed to buying groceries and cooking for yourself. It makes sense that the only items in your fridge would be a jar of mayonnaise, some cookie dough, and an extra large Taco Bell cup from three days ago. But you're not nineteen, you're twenty-seven years old and you have your own office. You've had eight years to learn how to boil water. Time's up. You lose.

Your Carbon Footprint

Are you kidding me? Take your styrofoam plate-using, recycle-refusing, incandescent light bulb-rocking, paper-towel-abusing, water-running, gas-guzzling, secondhand-smoke and methane-producing ass and get the fuck out of the farmer's market! Oh, and who brings a Big Mac to a farmer's market? Unbelievable.

Your Dirty Bathroom

Scientific studies show that there is a direct
correlation between the cleanliness of a
gentleman's sink and the cleanliness of his
balls. I, for one, do not dare question science.

Your Netflix Queue

Hmm, *The Butterfly Effect*, "Dave Matthews Band Live at Red Rocks," and something called "The Definitive Ryan Reynolds Collection." I think I'll stay in tonight and wash my hair, or more specifically, wash out the regret.

You Chew Tobacco

Oh wow, I see you've thought of everything. Champagne, strawberries, a clear plastic bottle filled with murky brown liquid? What is—Oh, fucking hell. Your spit bottle? Because you chew tobacco? Jesus. I thought it smelled like dead cowboys in here.

You Don't Like Prince

Get the fuck out of my Little Red
Corvette, Darling Nikki. Just know
that I Would Die 4 U, but no longer
do I Wanna Be Your Lover. I'm
leaving you, before you leave me,
standing in the Purple Rain, that is.
Why You Wanna Treat Me So Bad?

In conclusion, Batdance.

Your Posters

When the sun rose this morning and the light began to stream
through the blinds into your bedroom, I regained a sense of
clarity I was missing last night. Periodic Table of Liquor? Pink
Floyd's row of naked butts? Weed Leaf Tapestry? Kissing
Lesbians? If only I had the foresight to turn on a lamp.

You Left a Note

Big hurry, chief? Sure, I understand, we all have stuff to do, so I guess it's cool that you ducked out this morning before the sun came up. Although, I guess I'm just curious what you have to do that's so pressing on a Saturday morning? This note you left isn't really clearing anything up, either. *"Had to jet, but have a great day!"* Hmm, I could spend the rest of my weekend trying to decode that, but it doesn't take a language specialist to know that it really means: "look, I know I was bold enough to buy you drinks last night and go home with you and have sex with you all over every inch of your apartment, but the very thought of facing you in the sober light of daytime made me retreat to the hills." But thanks, I *will* have a great day!

Hey ___You___!

Name (If you can remember it)

Help yourself to a ___Toaster Strudel___ if you're feeling ___hungover___. Sorry to sneak

Leading Toaster Pastry   *Adjective*

out, but I had to run to ___spin class___. Last night was really ___special to me___,

Believable morning Obligation   *Lie*

and I think you're really ___cute___. I'd love to do it again soon, but the

Adjective describing favorite baby animal

next ___year___ is really ___apocalyptic___ for me. What with my

really long period of time   *Hyperbolically negative adjective*

___safari expedition___ and all. You should totally ___look me up on Myspace___.

Daunting and vague obligation   *Easily ignored means of social interaction*

<3, _____

Name/Fake Name

PS: Don't worry about ___the boner thing___, it happens to lots of ___dudes___.

Mortifying sex blunder   *Gender group*

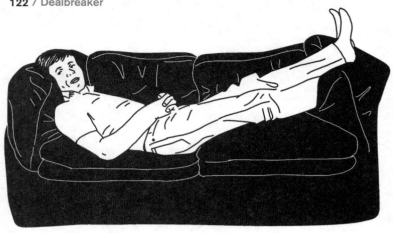

You Won't Leave

So, you don't have anywhere to be? Because I actually have
some plans. You want to just hang out here while I go to a
dentist appointment? You prefer to sit alone in my studio
apartment sifting through my magazines and college textbooks
and medicine cabinet and the top drawer of my nightstand
(seriously, stay the fuck out of there). That was kind of a
rhetorical question. Still flipping through my DVR and snacking
on my pita chips, eh? Don't you think you're getting a little
too comfortable with—yeah, those are my pajama pants. I
guess if you're uncomfortable you can—ah, you're going to
"grab a cat nap." Fuck. I guess I'll wake you when I get back in
eleven hours.

You Said "I Love You"

You don't love me. You can't love me. There's no way you can love someone based entirely on a modestly priced dinner (half-priced apps!), a moderately enjoyable movie (Ben Affleck!), and reasonably pleasurable sex (two different positions!). I liked you, that's for sure, but those new, warm-ish feelings turned to fear and dread as soon as you broke out the L word this morning. Come on, lady! At least play the game a LITTLE! Keep me guessing for a bit! Even if I felt the same way (which, after one night, I assure you, is impossible), I wouldn't break those three words for at least a month. Maybe two if I'm feeling especially cagey. It's a dizzy dance, this thing called love, and you've got two left feet. And they're facing the door.

Your Awesome Bed

Wow. I don't know what sort of memory foam, down-filled, Egyptian cotton, zillion thread count situation you have going on in here, but is it too soon to say that I could see myself spending a lot of time with you? Namely while sleeping, waking up, and sure, boning. Seriously though, how many mattress pads do you have? Is it one of those orange foam egg-crate things? Did you meet a genie in a faraway cave and this was what you wished for? Ah, fuck it, sometimes things this wonderful aren't meant to be understood.

You Make Me Delicious Pancakes

Hey, how long have you been up? Sorry, I was really tired. Oh my god, it smells amazing. What is this? How? Why? Just because? Because you know I love pancakes and I would probably be hungover and want breakfast? Holy shit. Never leave me.

Chapter 4

Three Months Later

*Who would have thought
that a serial dating,
commitment-phobic date
jumper like you would
be letting someone use your
toothbrush?*

Three weeks. Twenty-one days. Modern relationship math will tell you that this means roughly twelve to fifteen hangouts, with six to eight formal dates included in that figure. By now, if a couple has lasted this long, they've started to get a bit comfortable. Not too comfortable, mind you, but comfortable enough to start turning dates into "sleepovers," separate friends into mutual friends, and weekend morning-after see-you-laters into brunch and flea market Sundays.

And you've arrived here, at this amazing (and surprising) crossroads! Who would have thought that a serial dating, commitment-phobic date jumper like you would be letting someone use your toothbrush and not even batting an eye about it! You're hanging in there almost as long as Chevy Chase's foray into late night talk show hosting. Color us impressed, although you're not in the clear just yet.

Normally, there are a million and one reasons to bail on anyone you're seeing. Sometimes, however, these reasons are hiding under a façade of cool, a tricky crème brûlée skin that you can't crack in just twenty-one short days. No, you're going to have to delve a little deeper to uncover the secret hell that lurks within your seemingly great person. Perhaps you've been so blinded by the shockingly great sex that you failed to notice their incessant teeth grinding, or maybe their compliments seem so genuine that you've totally overlooked their unwillingness to let you choose a date location. Who knows?

Either way, some people require a little more detective work than just a cursory glance under the glow of barroom light. Sometimes you need to get in there with your infrared light like the CSI: Relationship lab technician we know you are. Put on those white powdery gloves and start poking around, you've got some emotional detective work to do.

Have your findings been conclusive? I sure hope so, because you've been puttering around in the lab for hours, and you look frustrated. I mean, there's only so many times you can dramatically rip off your sunglasses and spout hackneyed catchphrases before someone's going to notice something's wrong. Are you upset with your evidence, or worse yet, lack of evidence? Look, even the best scientists come up empty handed every now and then.

It's possible that in order to analyze your subject even further, you're going to have to dig a little deeper. A few more overnights, a few more dinners, and a dozen more drinks should do the trick. Listen, in no way should you take this as a defeat. In fact, be glad that you're not ready to donate this one to science so early in the game. Keep looking, because there's no telling what unknown horrors and scientific disasters lie beyond the first few weeks. This one might even be (gasp!) a keeper. Either way, if you've got the stomach for it, we're dying to know what happens.

You're Always Complaining

You're right, it is a little too hot. Why don't you take off your sweatshirt? Oh, I get it, you want me to turn the heat down. Done and done! What's that? Now you're too cold? Well, I can turn the heat back up—okay, I'll grab you a blanket then. We always just sit around and watch movies? What does that have to do with the temperature, you just—AHA! I see! This is a never-ending complaint vortex! If I don't escape, I will be perpetually in a state of listening to you be unhappy about things. The only way to avoid getting sucked down inside the vortex forever is to grab hold of something sturdy and never speak to you again.

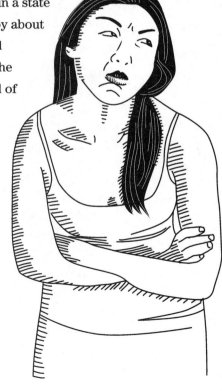

Your Unsolicited Advice

What's that, Dr. Phil? You think I'm just lashing out at you because I'm projecting my own deep-seated issues onto you, and you think I could benefit from a little perspective? And you think that despite my very high-paying job, I should go back to college and finish my degree, because I'm an "incomplete human" without it? That's a very interesting theory, and I'll take that under consideration, but I think I'd rather get psychological and spiritual guidance from someone I've known longer than three weeks, and who doesn't base their life's decisions around an inspirational wall calendar. Hang in there, indeed.

You Flirt with Other People

I know you think that what you're doing is just exhibiting your outgoing personality, and that you're a social butterfly, and that you can't help it if people just naturally gravitate toward you, and I guess that makes sense. However, if I could offer a counterpoint, I'd say this: your hand is down someone's pants, and that someone isn't me, and that's pretty hard to misconstrue. You slutty, slutty jerk.

Your Road Rage

Wow, what's with all this traffic? There must be an accident or something. Oh well, nothing to get too heated about, right? Like, not exactly a situation worthy of pounding on your steering wheel, shouting expletives out the window, honking your horn for fifteen seconds, or flipping off an... an ambulance? You just flipped off an ambulance? Oh boy. Well, this is my stop. Literally, figuratively, and otherwise.

Your Comic Sans

Our sexy e-mail correspondence isn't a children's birthday invitation. Deleted—from both my inbox and my life.

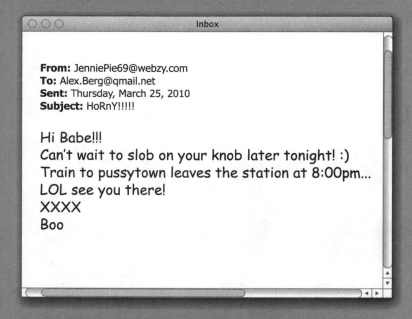

○ ○ ○   Inbox

From: JenniePie69@webzy.com
To: Alex.Berg@qmail.net
Sent: Thursday, March 25, 2010
Subject: HoRnY!!!!!

Hi Babe!!!
Can't wait to slob on your knob later tonight! :)
Train to pussytown leaves the station at 8:00pm...
LOL see you there!
XXXX
Boo

You're a Metrosexual

People stopped using this term in 2005. The novelty of an appearance-conscious man ended the day his girlfriend discovered he used her razor to "manscape." Take your ladies denim, "guyliner," and silky smooth skin (seriously, how do you get your skin so silky smooth?) and hit the road. Besides, I'm pretty sure in your case the term more accurately describes your tendency to give handjobs on the subway.

You're a Suicide Girl

No, Willow, I don't want to watch *Room Raiders* with you. I thought you were an alt chick, right? So let's do some *alt* stuff, okay? Take me to Trent Reznor's bondage party or something. That's what I want! Don't text me about what your cat did. You can't expect me to care that it drank milk. Do you get impressed when I drink milk? The boring bullshit to kinky sex ratio is all kinds of messed up. You're like the Girls Next Door, plus tattoos and piercings, minus the tan, plus antidepressants. I did not sign up for this.

You Only Drink Malternative Beverages

Here's what I think about it: sticky, artificially sweetened, tacky packaging, and leaves a bad aftertaste. Good for a go-around every now and then at a barbecue or a house party, but ultimately unsatisfying.

Oh, and that shit you're drinking is gross too.

You're a Furry

I would say, "it's not you, it's me," but I'm pretty sure we both know what's really going on.

You're a Doormat

Oh, so you're cool with anything? You literally have no opinion about where we should go to dinner? How about in a trash can? You want to eat garbage? Really? Of course, why would you care? Okay, well that's what we'll do. We will eat garbage out of a trash can. Do you want to catch a movie after dinner? Right, "whatever." How about that new movie *Drying Paint*? We can literally watch paint dry on a wall, but on a movie screen. Sounds great, does it? Perfect, I'll start the car.

You're a Vampire

No, you're not. You're not a vampire! Vampires don't take dates
to Olive Garden! Stop looking at me with your head tilted down
and your brow furrowed. I know you're trying to convey
smoldering intensity, but it actually just looks like you're
constipated. Also, did you put body glitter all over your face?
That's the dumbest thing I've ever seen, and I've seen the movie
Twilight. It doesn't matter that you "would lose control" if we
had sex, because that's not an option. You blew your chance
when your plastic fangs fell out of your mouth and landed in
your (never-ending) pasta bowl.

You're a Deadbeat

Look, times are tough. I get it. I know what it's like to be between jobs, but you haven't been employed in over a year. No, selling pot doesn't count. Especially not if you smoked it all. Work with me here! Also, I think you should stop banking on getting unemployment, unless you filled out tax information for your last job: recycling your old beer bottles. Let it be known that splitting a Pop-Tart from the vending machine in the laundry room does not a dinner date make.

P.S.: You owe me $600.

Your Creepy Roommate

Maybe it's my imagination, but it seems like your roommate knocks on the door and asks to borrow a DVD every time we have sex. It's always season three of *The Office*, and he only wants the first disc. Also, when he says, "you two sure look like you're having fun," I always feel like those are the last words I'm going to hear before I'm murdered.

You're Too Sensitive

All right, I'll give you a second. Do you want a Kleenex? You look sort of disgusting. Okay, sorry. It's just—your face is all puffy and snot-covered and you've been wiping your nose on your sleeve. Listen, man, you don't have to be a cowboy or anything, but this is getting out of control. If you're going to act like a baby every time your favorite sports team loses, or you catch the last 20 minutes of *Shawshank Redemption*, or when you get "overwhelmed by, like, life," well, this relationship just ain't big enough for the both of us.

You're Too Cute

This isn't working. I'm sorry, but I've tried
everything. Please, don't make this any
harder than it has to be. Just take your stuff
and go. Take your polka-dot underwear, your
cupcake tins, your Joanna Newsom vinyl, your Hello Kitty
lunch box, your sketchbook, your black leggings, your
melodica, your many plaid shirts, your Polaroid camera, your
enormous sunglasses, and your cat ears headband. No wait,
leave that. Now go back to the indie movie you came from and
leave me alone.

That Supercute Quirky Girl from That Movie

Fellas: We've got some bad news for you. The adorable female lead from your favorite quirky movie would be an obnoxious maniac if she were a real person. If we have to see one more movie where Natalie Portman or Zooey Deschanel play delicate little quirkmuffins, we'll probably enjoy it, buy the DVD, and start a Facebook group about it. But then we'd realize that those girls, also known as Manic Pixie Dream Girls, don't exist in reality, and their closest real-world approximations are usually total basket cases with daddy issues and a purse full of meds. Allow us to break the illusion for you and show you how shit would go down, real world vs. movie world.

Movie World: Supercute girl puts headphones on you and plays you a song that melts your little heart.

Real World: You've already heard the song, and you pretend to be impressed. However, she can see through it and gives you the silent treatment for the rest of the day.

Movie World: She tells you that you two are going for a ride. When you ask her where you're going, she puts a blindfold on you and says, "it's a secret." Then the two of you sneak into the natural history museum after hours and make out in the dinosaur room.

Real World: The secret place she takes you to is her coke dealer's house, and he makes you watch mildly pornographic movies where women fight each other.

Movie World: Cute girl invites you over to make a pillow fort. You two spend the evening eating s'mores under blankets and playing records, and then she dares you to kiss her!

Real World: Same scenario, but replace all the fun stuff with: the pillow fort reminds her of a traumatic childhood experience that she refuses to explain. You spend the rest of the night asking her if there's anything you can do while offering her a box of tissues.

Movie World: After an intense shared experience, this cute quirky girl cuts all of her hair off in an adorable pixie cut and begins speaking with a British accent because she's "starting over."

Real World: After chasing Xanax and Vicodin with a bottle of red wine, she shaves her head unevenly and passes out at your cousin's wedding.

Movie World: Your artsy, adorable, too-good-to-be-true crush constructs a scavenger hunt for you with step-by-step instructions. You have to take a picture of a smiling baby, find a cloud that looks like a sleeping lion, and release five balloons into the air. The final step of the scavenger hunt takes you to a rooftop, where your favorite indie band plays a private concert for the two of you.

Real World: She kills herself.

There it is, guys. Quirky and adorable movie girls may not exist in real life, but look at it this way, at least Zach Braff hasn't directed a movie since 2004.

You're a Problem Drunk

"Hey Caitlin, this is Sherriff Mike Brown, again. We have Tyler here at the station in custody for public intoxication. He was arrested after instigating an argument at the Taco Town on Spring Street. Tyler reportedly attempted to climb over the counter into the kitchen, insisting he make his own burrito. When the employees tried to restrain him, he responded by shouting 'boy's night out!' The record states Tyler was alone."

You Don't Listen To Me

So, I thought maybe later we could hit up my friend's party. It's going to be smallish, but we could always bail if it's not fun. If it's dead, there's always the bar, but it's usually so packed on Fridays. Maybe we could stay in and watch a movie? Huh? Sounds good? What sounds good? I just gave you three options. Put down your nail file. Because I'm talking to you! Yes? Yes what, I didn't ask a question! Holy shit, you're not listening to me at all. We need to talk! HELLO?? Hello? Oh my god. Well, I'm just going to go outside and pull the sun out of the sky and break it apart with my bare hands. You know, because that's something I can do, and always have been able to do. Because I'm a superhero. And an alien. And I'm made of magic, and my butt shoots laser beams. Nothing huh? I guess nothing will ever be as interesting as the monkey clanging cymbals that lives inside your head.

Your Baby Talk

I am not, nor will I ever be, your Shmoo.

You're a Scientologist

"Hey, sugar! I'll be out of the meeting at around seven thirty, so let's plan on getting dinner at eight. Are you feeling okay? You seem really stressed lately, and my friend Giovanni says that's totally curable. Can I borrow $15,000? Also, do you believe in aliens?"

You're Not Into That Sex Thing I'm Into

Yeah, ha ha. I was just joking about wanting to try that. Unless
you weren't? You were? Okay, whatever. Cause if you weren't, I
mean, I am totally open-minded. It's not like it's weird or
anything. No, it's not weird. We are adults, and we should feel
comfortable expressing ourselves. Please stop laughing. Please.
Please stop laughing and hand me my bra.

You Remind Me of My Dad

Funny, this picture of us at Disneyland is the spitting image of a similar picture from when I was a little kid, see! It was my seventh birthday and my dad surprised me with the trip; it was great! Yeah, I guess that's sort of the same thing you did, surprising me on my birthday... Huh. Weird, you guys have the same name, too. Hmm, yeah, you sort of do look similar here... Well, maybe it's only your beards. And you both have wavy dark hair. And he's wearing basically the exact same outfit as you in this picture. And the way you both have your arm around me in that protective way... well, maybe it's just in the picture, that makes sense! Although, you both make really dumb puns all the time. And you both give me a hard time about dropping out of college. And you're both really fiscally conservative, and you have the same terrible taste in TV shows. And you both have a tendency to get condescending. And you both have antiquated ideas about the role of women in the household. Look, I know a lot of girls are drawn to men that remind them of their fathers, and that's why I'm rebelling against this! That's why this is over. And if you want a more interesting reason, if you were ever to meet my dad face-to-face, it would probably alter the space-time continuum, and you know what that means: Dinosaurs come back, Hitler is somehow president, daily earthquakes, and assorted other forms of destruction and chaos. Looks like It's back in the DeLorean for you.

You're a Gamer

Are you sure you don't want to come to bed? It's 4AM and I could really use some sleep without hearing you yelling at 13-year-old boys in Japan on your spaceman headset to "guard your rear!" Ugh, get those joystick-calloused hands and your Fanta-stained lips away from me. No, we aren't fucking on your videogame rocking chair, I don't care if it vibrates or has a cup holder. Why would *that* matter? When your ass falls asleep after remaining stationary for 4 hours, that's not your body's design flaw, it's nature's way of telling you to emerge from your sweaty den of button-mashing. I'm going back to sleep. In my own bed.

You're a Momma's Boy

You know, I like a guy who has a good relationship with his mother; my own mom once said that it's an indicator of how a man will treat all the women in his life. She didn't, however, mention what is indicated by answering phone calls from her while we are fucking. Or running every decision by her, from which color to paint your living room to what to make for breakfast. Or needing her permission before dating a girl or else there is no chance for this to work out. There is only room for one lady in this relationship, try not to trip over your umbilical cord on the way out.

Your Love of Cocaine

ohmygodilovethissongtooandithinkwetotallyhavearealconnectio
nbutyouretalkingreallyclosetomyfaceandyouregrittingyourteeth
andwhileyouredealingwithanosebleedimgoingtoslipoutthedoor.

Your Constant Check-Ins

The following text messages were sent between 6:45PM and 7:05PM

Thinking of you! :) XOXO

Wish you were here LOL

Whatcha doin?

We still on for movies later?

Hey, just checking in, seeing what u r up to

You there??? :(

SRSLY I'm getting worried :(((

HELLO!!!! are you mad at me?

Please txt me back.

PLZ PLZ PLZ baby I miss you!!!

PLZ txt me back :((((((

OK FINE FUCK U

YOU ASSHOLE

YOU FUCKING COCKSUCKER

HOW DARE U BLOW ME OFF

FUCK U WE ARE DONE

I'm soooooo sorry I didnt mean it!!!

I MISS YOU !!!!! :(((((

PLEASE CALL ME NOW

My phone was off... and now I'm never going to answer it again.

♥DEALMAKERS

You Volunteer to Give Me Back Massages

Sorry, I'm sort of in a shitty mood. My boss made me put together all these IKEA shelves and it took forever, and now I'm sore and exhausted. All right, sure, we can hug. Wait, what are you doing? What is happening? Oh. My. God. Oh. My. God. Ohmygodohmygodohmygodohmygodohmygodohmygodohmygod. Do this forever.

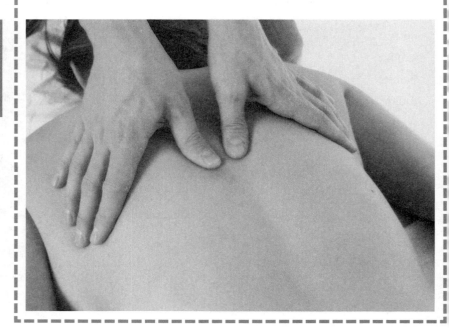

You're So Fucking Talented

Hey, I know I'm early, but I was in the neighborhood. Oh, that's cute, you were painting in your living room. Sure, I'd like to see—probably a bowl of fruit or a sunset or something. Holy shit. You painted this? You painted this today? You fucking woke up and fucking painted this? Jesus Christ, I need to sit down. Sure, I would like something to eat. Probably some cereal or something. Jesus Christ. You made this? You used fucking herbs and spices and seasonings and and threw this together? Fuck! Yeah, maybe some music would help me relax.. You are sitting in front of a piano. You have a fucking piano? You are smiling at me and sitting at a piano, and magic is coming from your hands, you are not wearing a bra, and you are covered in paint from this fucking painting you just fucking painted. Consider my chips cashed in.

Chapter 5

Three Months Later

You've swapped enough pajamas, DVDs, and books to make any separation at the very least an inconvenience.

Well well well, what do we have here? These months have
flown by, and before you knew it, you've found yourself in a full-
blown, bona fide relationship. After all, relationships are
measured by increments of three months. The first three is
halfway to six, which is halfway to a whole year, which is
practically the same as one foot over the finish line: Marriage?
Death? Who knows. At this point, you stop counting anyway.
You finally introduce your partner as your significant other rather
than simply by name, and when they're not around you no
longer refer to them as someone you're "you know, well,
hanging out with, but whatever."

At this notch on the commitment timeline, sleepovers have
become a more-often-than-not. You've swapped enough
pajamas, DVDs, and books to make any separation at the very
least an inconvenience. You enjoy each other's constant
company enough to go on a weekend-out-of-town/road trip/visit
to a winery. Spare toothbrushes have earned habitual spots
beside the sink. A parent comes into town to visit, and you're

more than happy to plan an introduction. That first little
squabble (well it certainly *looked* like you were flirting) was
quickly resolved by a long awaited surrender to that
conversation where someone, aided by alcohol or not, spills
those vulnerable beans about how they are, "only getting so
worked up about this because they really really really like you."
Finally!

By this point, your friends have certainly taken notice. Suddenly
you, the once self-proclaimed Party Machine, are absent from
outings all together: missing from the last call at bars, the
sweaty grinding dance floors, the 3AM pancake houses with
strangers. You can't even remember the last time you got
blackout drunk! Is it possible that your balls-deep partying was
a masqueraded quest for a soul mate? All those tequila shots
and bathroom hookups were merely preliminary steps toward
the ultimate goal of having someone with whom to stay home,
cook dinner, share a bottle of wine and fall asleep on the couch
watching a movie? It certainly feels that way, with the way the
past three months have been going. After all, there is a comfort
in not having to participate in the dating rat race. Your single
friends envy your newfound stability, and your couple friends
rejoice at having another pair of members for their dinner party
club. Your mother is already planning on setting an extra place

at Thanksgiving. Everyone is rooting for you to defy your relationship history and make it work—barring a few intolerable characteristics, that is.

The three-month mark, along with its snugglefests and impending stability, comes with a footnote. Little, critical mental notes that sprinkle over these cherished memories like a garbage garnish. They could be small qualities that irk you at first but then snowball into suitcase-packing fits of rage down the road. Or, they fizzle out altogether, only to become part of the collage of adorable eccentricities of your beloved. Worst of all, you could come to the brutal realization that this person who you have been naked with three to five times a week is not, at all, who you previously assumed. An impostor. A charlatan. A total gross, awful weirdo who you can't even believe you were so crazy about considering how fucking gross and awful they are. Gross. Disgusting! What a mistake... you know, or not!

You Can't Hang

No, we can't leave yet. Why? Because we just got here! How are you tired? It's 9:30PM! This is my best friend from college! I've known him for ten years! Ugh, why does that deserve an eye roll? Of course you don't know anyone at this party. They're all old friends of mine who've been dying to meet you! You always bail on me when I meet up with them. What? "You have enough friends?" Wow. No, I won't give you cab fare, you're staying! Of course, you'll have things to say to them. Don't assume you have nothing in common with them just because—oh no, put down that bottle. I swear, if you ruin another social function with your red wine coma, I will leave you here. I will leave you wherever you collapse. Goddamnit. If I knew you were going to act like a baby, I would have left you with a sitter.

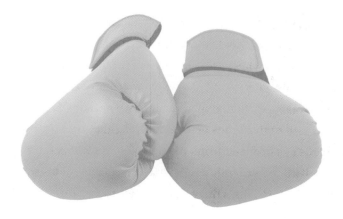

You're Always Picking Fights

No, it's cool if we get Japanese food tonight. Yeah, I know it's not my favorite but you like it and I'll find something I like on the menu. No, I'm not being agreeable just to be agreeable, I'm actually just hungry and I don't want to sit here for an hour and—AHA!!! WOW!! Nice try! I can't believe I almost fell for it! The old "turn a harmless conversation into a fight" trick. Man! You're good. You're really good. You're like a magician, but instead of pulling rabbits out of hats, you're amazing at turning a normal conversation into an argument with a single wave of your magic temper! I have a suggestion for your next magic trick: how about you chill the fuck out for a minute?

You Don't Reciprocate Oral Sex

Esteemed associate, Weekly Co-habitator. I have called you here today to address a very serious concern that threatens the harmony of this alliance. It has come to my attention that there is a trade imbalance in this relationship. We have been exporting fellatio at rate of five times per week, while import of cunnilingus has dropped from one time per week to zero times per week with the exception of a birthday. If eighteenth-century economist Adam Smith's theory on absolute advantage has taught us anything, ignoring this deficit can only result in one thing: You're going to get dumped for a dude who's begging to chomp on this box lunch.

You Always Want to Stay In

Dinner and a DVD. Dinner, DVD. Dinner. DVD. DVD, Dessert?
Wow! Way to go out on a limb for this relationship. You really
tossed me a curveball with that pint of Rocky Road, didn't you?
This totally makes up for the fact that you haven't wanted to go
to any of the parties, concerts, comedy shows, art galleries,
lectures, theme parks, Renaissance fairs, or flash mobs I've
invited you to for the past three months. If you should ever
become curious as to what lies outside of your apartment door,
wonder no longer: It's me.

You Love Strip Clubs

Listen, I am a "cool girlfriend." If we are partying in Vegas and you want a lap dance, I will gladly cheer you on or even giggle my way through my own. However, you're spending $600 a night to have a lady of questionable background and obvious motherhood clank her shoes together and coax you into buying her $12 sodas. If you prefer your naked women to come with a price tag, your bill is in the mail.

Your Public Displays of Affection

Craig, this has been a great lunch. One question: is the unlimited soup, salad, and breadsticks supposed to come with a public fingerbang?

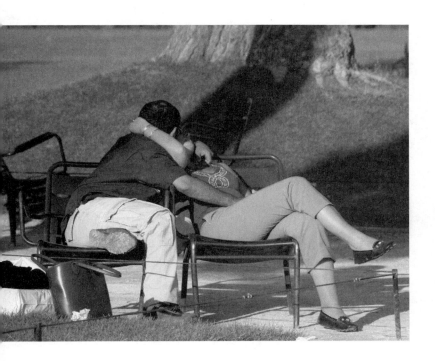

You're Probably a Lesbian

"Hey, sweetie! Listen, if you don't mind I'm going to bail on our picnic today. Don't hate me, I just forgot that I promised my friend from work that we'd go to the flea market. You remember her, right? She's that petite blond girl from my office? Totally cute style? Anyway, she and I are probably going to do girl stuff after the flea market. It's nothing you'd be into, don't worry! Just probably some yoga, maybe some red wine, stuff like that. Also I think she and I are road tripping to San Fran together just for fun! And you know how times are tough right now, so I'm gonna move in with her to save on rent. So practical! Anyway, I promise I'll make it up to you later this week. Love ya!"

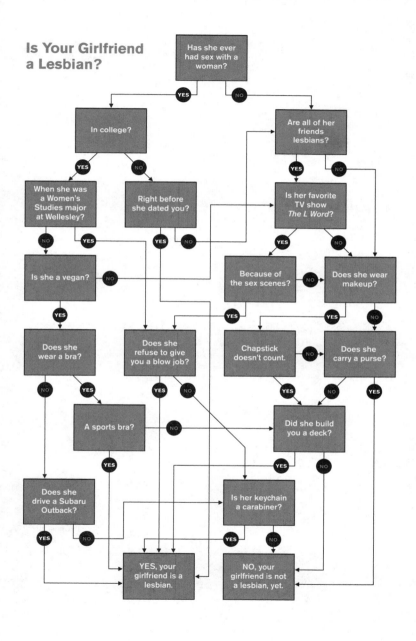

Is Your Girlfriend a Lesbian?

Has she ever had sex with a woman?

YES → **In college?**

NO → **Are all of her friends lesbians?**

In college?
YES → **When she was a Women's Studies major at Wellesley?**
NO → **Right before she dated you?**

Are all of her friends lesbians?
YES → **Is her favorite TV show *The L Word*?**
NO → **Does she wear makeup?**

When she was a Women's Studies major at Wellesley?
NO → **Is she a vegan?**
YES → (down)

Right before she dated you?
YES → (down)
NO → **Is her favorite TV show *The L Word*?**

Is her favorite TV show *The L Word*?
YES → **Because of the sex scenes?**
NO → **Does she wear makeup?**

Is she a vegan?
NO → (right)
YES → **Does she wear a bra?**

Because of the sex scenes?
NO → **Does she wear makeup?**
YES → **Does she refuse to give you a blow job?**

Does she wear makeup?
YES → **Chapstick doesn't count.**
NO → **Does she carry a purse?**

Does she wear a bra?
NO → (down)
YES → **A sports bra?**

Does she refuse to give you a blow job?
YES → (down)
NO → **Did she build you a deck?**

Chapstick doesn't count.
NO → **Does she carry a purse?**
YES → **Did she build you a deck?**

Does she carry a purse?
NO → **Did she build you a deck?**
YES → (down)

A sports bra?
NO → **Did she build you a deck?**
YES → **Does she drive a Subaru Outback?**

Did she build you a deck?
YES → **Is her keychain a carabiner?**
NO → (down)

Does she drive a Subaru Outback?
YES → (down)
NO → **YES, your girlfriend is a lesbian.**

Is her keychain a carabiner?
YES → **YES, your girlfriend is a lesbian.**
NO → **NO, your girlfriend is not a lesbian, yet.**

YES, your girlfriend is a lesbian.

NO, your girlfriend is not a lesbian, yet.

Your Best Friend Is Your Ex

I love our game nights! It's great that that we can open up our home to our closest friends for some good old-fashioned fun. But, it's kind of strange that your ex always ends up on the invite list. And always shows up. And brings a snack that somehow references a fond, shared memory. And that you two miraculously wind up on the same team. Every, single, time. Yup, lots of whispering (with ear cupping!), conspiring, giggling, and scheming when it's time to decide on those important Trivial Pursuit answers. Here's a question: what twenty-first century couple broke up famously over a game of Trivial Pursuit?

Your Delusions of Grandeur

Yes, I sure will move to LA/New York/Chicago/Portland/San Francisco with you so you can follow your dreams! Yes, I think you'd make a great singer/songwriter/actor/poet/novelist/installation artist/animal trainer/stand-up comedian/botanist/revolutionary. No I'm not being sarcastic! My voice just does this when I'm being really, really sincere with the one who I love so dearly and believe in so unconditionally. Am I laughing? I'm laughing aren't I? I can't even tell anymore.

You're Lazy

HEAR HEAR!! ALL HAIL THE KING OF MOTIVATION, MASTER OF TASK COMPLETION! For our loyal leader managed to put on pants (covered in mustard stains) take a shower (spray-cologne your armpits) and leave the house (to buy weed)! No, I don't want breakfast, it's four in the afternoon. Are you falling asleep while I'm talking to you? If you need to take a cat nap, you can curl up in the litter box for a while. Unsubtle version: You're a real piece of shit.

You're Bananas

Please calm down. PLEASE! Okay, at some point I'm going to ask you to replace that picture frame. Not now, but eventually. Now, let me apologize for the fourth time, I'm sorry. I didn't know that you had a weird thing with a guy who sounded like an old southern gentleman. I was just doing a funny voice. I was trying to make you laugh—STOP THROWING THINGS!! PLEASE! I'M RUNNING OUT OF THINGS! Do you want a ride to CVS? I DON'T KNOW, maybe because you finished both of your prescriptions and haven't refilled them in a week. That's not a good reason to throw rice at me! Where did you get rice! You have successfully thrown everything there is to throw in this apartment except the dog. Don't even think about it. Back away from the beagle. Why don't you go lie down for a while? I'll clean it up. If only I could tidy up your brain with a broom, I would.

You Don't Believe in Evolution

Learning this information about you guarantees we will not procreate. How's that for evidence of natural selection?

Your Sugar Daddy

So, we can't hang out tonight because you're going to an art gallery with Philip? And who is Philip? Oh, he's a fifty-six-year-old man who pays your rent in exchange for "companionship"? Oh. Oh, okay. You know, when you use air quotations while saying the word "companionship," you sort of open the floodgates for a conversation involving handjobs. Anyway, tell Phil to remember to take his heart medicine. Have fun!

Your Checkered Past

I thought that mug shot I found of you was a novelty picture from a photo booth or a state fair. I thought that guy at the Dodgers game who kept calling you Lisa was just a crazy person, especially when he kept screaming, "You burned my house down, Lisa!" But when they wouldn't let us into Disneyland because they claimed you were banned for life, that's when I knew something was wrong. I mean, really, who tries to deal coke while waiting in line for Space Mountain? Bad people, that's who.

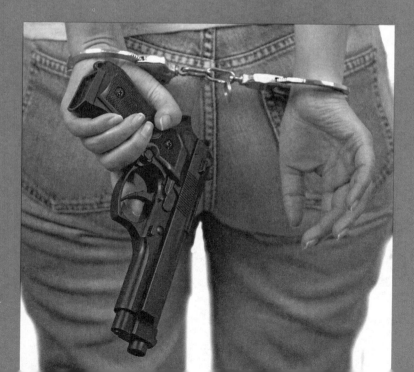

You Treat 4/20 as a Holiday

No, I didn't know that 7-Eleven sells omelet taquitos. I hope you're aware that saying you're "taking a day off work" doesn't mean anything if you don't have a job.

Your Grammar

they're / their / there

your / you're

its / it's

For example:

You're not getting a BJ. It's over. There is the door.

You're an Idiot

Wow, you're beautiful. I could look at you all day, just please stop talking. Everything you say is a tiny dagger into the heart of my attraction for you. Don't ask me what state New York City is in unless you're kidding. Don't tell the lady at the burrito stand that you don't speak "Mexican," it's inaccurate and racist. Do you even. Oh my god. How do you not know what BLT stands for? Are you an alien? Stop it. No, I'm not going to explain how John Mayer got inside of your iPod shuffle. That was it. That was the last straw. Enjoy your successful modeling career.

Your Daddy Issues

No, I'm not going to leave you. I'm just going to the kitchen… to get a glass of water. See? You can see the kitchen from the couch. Just keep looking at me. Still here! I'm not going anywhere, I promise! Except maybe back to my apartment, eventually! What. What did I say? Well, of course I'm going home at some point, I live there, and that's where my clean clothes are. "Typical"? How is that typical? Oh, right, your dad worked late and was always away on business. I don't see how that's my problem, but it does explain why you made me wear this gray wig and cardigan. I probably should have questioned that earlier, but I've done weirder things to get laid before. Please feel free to take your need for older male attention elsewhere, like the YMCA or the duck pond. Or Craigslist.

You're Sketchy

Is that a pager? Who still has a pager? Right, doctors. I'm pretty
sure you're not a doctor because I don't know of any doctors
who also work at Best Buy. Also, your jacket has too many
pockets. I can't trust a man who has that many pockets. What's
your angle? Who are you? Sure, I'm enjoying this dinner, but
you keep getting up from the table every five minutes to "check
your voice mail." Also, why do you keep whispering to the
busboy? You're either planning to propose to me in some
elaborate way, or sell me several grams of uncut cocaine.
Neither of those things interest me.

You Won't Talk to Me in Public

So, I'm not hallucinating, right? We are dating each other? I mean, I hope I'm not just losing my mind, because we *did* come here together in the same car. From the same apartment? After having the same sex together? It's just weird that you're standing all the way on the other side of this party, talking to a really good-looking person, and avoiding eye contact with me. You know, call me crazy, but you seem like you don't want people to know about us! I think what tipped me off was when we were in the car and you said, "I don't want people to know about us."

You're Imaginary

You are great, ok? It's not like you're not amazing, that's not the problem. You're smart; you're sensitive; you're caring; you're hot (haha, sorry I had to say it!); you know how to cook; you give me space when I need it; your friends are cool; you can always make me laugh; you're a humanitarian but you're not pious or obnoxious about it; you're amazing in bed (seriously, where did you learn that?); you're in good shape, yet you aren't a crazy gym fanatic who takes weird supplements and has creepy veins; and best of all, you genuinely seem to love me. Literally the only problem with you is that I'm imagining you. What gives you the right to not exist?

Your Clumsy Threesome Propositions

"Hey, you. So, uh, you know that girl from my acting class? Right, right, Kim. Well, she's coming over later and like, she's gonna run lines with me for an hour or two. Is that cool? I mean, it'll only take a while, and like, she's gonna bring by a bottle of wine or whatever. You're totally welcome to have some, I mean. Look, I'm not kicking you out when she comes over. You should stay, totally. I mean, she wants you. I mean, she wants you to stay. Kim! You remember Kim, right? From the thing? With the great skin? I mean white skin. Shit, let me start over. I want to have sex with you and Kim. UGHHHH, no. No no no! Come baaaaaaaack!"

So, You Want to Have an Orgy

Pulling off a threesome is not easy. Neither is finding a unicorn or a leprechaun or a puppy that's born housebroken. Not easy even in the slightest, no sir. But if you have an imagination that's capable of being stretched, this feat isn't quite so impossible. All you need is a little ingenuity, a hope, a prayer, and a lot of luck. In fact, you'll need more than a little luck. You'll need all the face-up pennies, crossed fingers, and 11:11's in the world to bring you that much closer to a two-partner pileup.

In order to set up a successful threesome, the stars need to align. You need to be in an ideal relationship (or an agreement that resembles a relationship) with an ideal person, and your third party needs to be willing, able, and approved by all participants. Basically, you need to lead a charmed existence, which is not something one can easily fabricate. So short of scouring Polyamory seminars and the back pages of your local free newspaper, it's pretty hard to pull off a threesome.

So, maybe what you need to do is have yourself an orgy! Eh? Why not? Why stop at one superfluous partner when you can have literally dozens of strangers all up in your personal parts/business? It's going to be a lot easier to find people that are REALLY weird than just a bit freaky, because the supercreeps aren't into playing coy. They'll let you know right off the bat that they're into the nutty shit. If you're going to get weird, get really weird! Live on the very outermost fringes of societal norms! You'll be one step away from receding to the woods, only to be seen twenty-five years later when HBO's *Real Sex 467* comes to your commune to capture your aged lovemaking techniques for posterity. Here are ten surefire tips to planning and/or pulling off a successful sex party.

► Start wearing your shirts unbuttoned to the chest.

► Ladies: you too.

► Hang out at couples-only dinner parties and see who bites (figuratively and literally).

► Buy cologne. You'll need it. You won't think you will, but you will.

► Stockpile boxed wine.

► Get rid of any furniture you're particularly attached to. Instead, invest in some tasteful air mattresses.

► Make sure all guests monogram their robes (to avoid confusion).

► Don't have kids. If you have kids, be prepared to have the kind of kids that run away from home, cook meth in a trailer, and eat people in prison.

▶ Start winking suggestively in casual conversation. You'll increase your chances of meeting a POP* (*Potential Orgy Participant) ten fold!

▶ Invest in clothing with flames, dragons, and anything else that could possibly bring to mind magic.

▶ And finally, buy some scented candles. Buy some air fresheners. Some citronella coils, maybe. Grab a window fan or two. Get a nice cross breeze going. Light some incense. Install a screen door. If you don't, anyone and everyone who comes to your house after this sex party is going to smell something, and even though they're not going to be able to identify it, you can be sure they're not going to like it. Enjoy!

You're Almost Awesome

You're like a three-course meal that ends with a bland dessert. You're a really gripping movie that just sort of falls apart in the third act. You're a too-good-to-be-true tropical vacation cut short by food poisoning. You're a Lisa-heavy episode of *The Simpsons*. You're a graceful salsa dance punctuated by a poorly timed fart. You're so close to perfection, and yet so fart away. That fart pun, on the other hand, was absolutely flawless.

My Parents Love You

My mom is the high priestess of judgment, and my dad's a notorious hard ass. Both of them are impossible to please and beyond critical no matter who I bring home. And yet, within mere minutes of meeting you, they're laughing, beaming, and flashing me barely concealed and moderately mortifying thumbs-up signs. I don't know if you're a mind control expert or some kind of voodoo doctor, but whatever you're doing, keep doing it. If the people that made me are in love with you, I guess there's no reason I shouldn't be as well. At the very least, I should keep you around long enough to make future family gatherings a little more tolerable.

This Is Actually Working

Okay, what's your game? You're nice, smart, funny, attentive, and you want to be around me as much as I want to be around you? Is this a trap? I think I deserve to know, so at least I'll have a context for all this happiness I'm feeling. Who do you think you are? You think you can just waltz right into somebody's life and then go right ahead and remind them that the world isn't as much of a cold, joyless place as they had previously concluded? You think you can make me feel all these feelings that were very deliberately kept under lock and key? You think you can sidle up right beside me on this sofa and give me a hug so reassuring, so comforting, even my cynical heart is assured that everything is going to be all right? Well, you're right, you can.

Chapter 6

The Breakup and Beyond

All the Chicken Parm and BJs in the world aren't going to change the fact that the fat lady's singing.

Emotions tend to build up to a boil at the end of even the most awful relationships. Breakups are difficult for both parties. Even if someone is really disgusting, it's never fun to hurt someone's feelings. That's why you must remain strong in the face of a breakup. The guilt, the blame, the self-reflection (must we accept our destiny as forever single and caring for more than the acceptable amounts of cats?) are in full swing for the weeks or even months following the breakup. Stumbling home from a bar and wanting a warm body to spoon does not warrant the late night drunk text message. A grocery store run-in does not warrant a coffee date, and certainly not a "let's try to be friends, and if we end up making out in one of our cars, so be it" (one of the most oft-repeated phrases in the history of breakups).

It was you who pulled the plug, remember? Because they are so unbearable to be with? Stick to your guns and recall the reasons you kicked that dud to the curb to begin with. And if those aren't holding up in your last-call loneliness, we dare you to give it another shot. It's only a matter of time until this whole new arrangement implodes under the weight of casually seeing other people and no-strings-attached sex. Sometimes you really need to heed those warning signs and admit defeat. It's over, and even if it's not done yet, it's damn close.

The final nails are sliding into the coffin, and even though you're holding the hammer, you can't deny you're getting wistful for the early days. Remember the trips to the mall? Remember looking at the cute baby animals at the pet store? You didn't care that those dogs came from a puppy mill! Remember going to shitty movies earlier this year? You didn't care that tickets were expensive and that it starred Jason Statham, you still paid full price for it. Those days, however, are long gone by now. Those fond memories have been replaced by reluctance to meet the parents, hushed arguments at housewarming parties, and sex so infrequent that you're actually starting to forget what each other's bodies look like.

These are clear indicators that the end is nigh. Sure, you can make your last ditch attempts to save this thing. You can rent some movies and cook some dinners and perform all the oral sex your special someone can handle. Unfortunately for you, all the Chicken Parm and BJs in the world aren't going to change the fact that the fat lady's singing. Yes sir, it's over. Maybe you got too comfortable, perhaps one of you is cheating, or maybe you're both just secretly sick of each other. It's probably time to cut your losses and move on.

This is the end, my only friend. The end. It's called a breakup, not a drag-this-out-forever-until-both-parties-want-to-murder-each-other up. You can say "everything happens for a reason" and get into Yoga and reinvent yourself until you're perfect for your next suitor, or you can say "fuck it" and have a few drawn-out months of ex-sex that ends with a new breakup that makes the first one look like a picnic in comparison. If you've been reading this entire book looking for the right answer, we'll give it to you. This whole book has been building up to this one sentence. It's going to tie everything together, and you're going to be so glad you read the whole thing. Are you ready? Here it is:

There's no right answer.

There it is. Do you feel cheated? Slighted? Used? Abused? Do you want your money back?

We hope not. Because if you've gone looking for the answers to life's many questions in a humor book, you've got bigger problems than just dating woes. There's really no right way to go about dealing with each individual relationship you might be confused by. We oversimplify as human beings, and so we've gone ahead and made it easy to label everyone you're dating, want to date, or have dated in the past as a hideous monster. It's called putting a Band-Aid on a problem, and it feels a lot better than the alternative: lots of ice cream, pajamas, and the knowledge that you've transformed into a living, breathing Cathy cartoon. If you can move on and realize that you have more than enough worth as a person to validate your own existence long enough to find someone else, you'll be just fine. Let us remind you that your last breakup happened for a few very good reasons. Okay? Hey, are you texting? Wait a minute. PUT THAT PHONE AWAY! You're better than that. Read this chapter. Don't you DARE send a text! Do you have any idea what time it is? Have you been drinking? You're not even listening to me! You're going to regret this! Give me your phone. HEY! What did I say? Read this last chapter while we go looking for a really good place to hide this thing. Unbelievable.

You Dumped Me

No, I don't want to help you move, assemble an end table, or even go to a romantic bed-and-breakfast with you. We are not together, that's why! You dumped me because you didn't want to see or talk to me anymore, remember? Because it wasn't "working for you anymore"? Well, this little seesaw you call an arrangement isn't exactly working for me either, darling. I appreciate you throwing some emotional and poorly timed sex my way, though. While it's happening, I am not even thinking about "us," and it's great. Although, I know that as soon as it ends, you'll tell me that if I stay, it'll become "too real." The phrase "confusing gray area" always sounds better when you're naked. Look, this isn't a revolving door. I'm the bouncer at this club from now on, and I say no reentry. You're either in or out, and "out" means I'm not feeding your fish anymore.

Your Horrible Excuses to See Me

Hello? What? No, I mean, yes. You did wake me up, I guess. Sorry, I'm really tired and out of it and what did you want again? Your watch? Watts? Are you saying Watch or Watts? OH! SWATCH? You're saying Swatch? As in a tacky wristwatch? You think you left it at my place? Please slow down. I honestly, seriously doubt that your watch is—SORRY, SWATCH. I highly doubt it's here. I'll check, but I don't really remember seeing a Swatch, and this is kind of a tiny apartment—Oh, you want to come check yourself? Right now? Well, seeing as you're crying right now, I don't think that's such a good idea. Oh, it's a bad phone connection and it only SOUNDS like you're crying and whining about getting back together. Okay, well here's another reason. It's 4:30AM, which you'd know if you didn't lose your fucking Swatch!

You Moved On REALLY Fast

Oh hey. I'm a little stunned to see you, actually. It's only been two weeks since we broke up and I guess I'm still reeling from it a little bit. I'm doing well, just working a lot and, uh, doing a lot of, you know, what's that on your finger? NOT THAT FINGER, although that looks like soy sauce. YOUR RING FINGER! It's a ring! A fucking ring! Please tell me that was a result of an expedition to the bottom of a Cracker Jack box and not a whirlwind jaunt down marathon romance street. I mean, I'm STILL moving stuff out of your place. Who are you engaged to? One of my movers??? OH sweet Jesus. I feel like I've been hit by the irony truck, backed over, and flattened again. If you need me I'll be spending half the time we were together trying to get over you. Enjoy getting married, and by that I mean, fuck everything.

You Won't Let This Be Over

"If you love someone, set them free"

—*Richard Bach*

"When one door closes,
another door opens"

—*Alexander Graham Bell*

"We broke up 2 months ago,
so stop showing up at my
office holding carnival-sized
teddy bears and upsetting my
coworkers with your out-of-control
sobbing. No, I don't need my copy of *Eat,
Pray, Love* back. And, please, change your
Facebook status back to single."

—*Me, Your Rational Ex, who clearly made the
right decision*

The Freeze Out

Have you ever pulled a freeze out? A freeze out is when you intentionally ignore or avoid someone electronically in order to get them to pay attention to you. It requires an icy exterior, an iron will, and the drive to keep going no matter what. It also doesn't really work, so it helps to be a little bit stupid, too.

The rules are simple: no texting, no e-mailing, no messaging, and no Facebooking. Usually performed in the wake of a breakup, the middle of a hiatus of some kind, or somewhere inside of a weird amorphous thing that has gone awry along the way, this tactic is not terribly effective because if you're not getting in touch with someone, it's impossible to show that you actually want their attention. It's counterintuitive, and it can sometimes seem like you might be better off trying to psychically will the person to get in touch with you.

"I don't care about you. In fact, I'm being totally chill just hanging out here on the Internet, talking to all sorts of awesome people, and wouldn't you just love to be one of them?" That's what you hope the green circle next to your Gchat name will convey. But you're wrong. All that it really conveys is, "I'm currently using an online messaging service that is tied to my e-mail account." It means you're available to talk online, and the person you're trying to freeze out is not doing anything with that knowledge. "Wait just a second," says the unreliable detective that lives in your brain. "Maybe they're freezing YOU out!" Panic sets in. Never thought of that, did you? Could your nemesis be as sinister as you? If so, you're left with one option: get the fuck out of Dodge, cowboy. Sign off!

It seems as though the best a freeze out can do is earn you a "hey, what's up? It's been a long time!" However, the worst it can do is get you a one-way ticket to a double freeze out, resulting in months of uncommunicative silence. Is it really worth the gamble? Is it really worth the uncertainty? You're playing with emotional gunpowder, and a poorly timed explosion could earn you a trip to the Apple Store with a coffee mug stuck angrily into your laptop.

So, the moral of the story is this: if you find yourself sitting in front of your computer late at night, slightly drunk (or even worse, completely sober), and you're contemplating sending an ill-advised instant message to break the long silence, don't. Just do what normal people do: sign off and go look at 400 of someone's Facebook pictures. True, it's less active, and, true, you're putting a stop to the sexy game of Internet cat and mouse you've deluded yourself into thinking you're in the middle of. Think of it this way: it's infinitely less sad than playing e-chicken with someone who probably doesn't care enough to get out of the way.

You're a Bad Breaker-Upper

I admire your attempt to rhyme "treasure" with "closure," but like most things about this relationship, your poem just misses the mark. Look, I know you have a lot of feelings, and you're hoping not to hurt mine, but reading an original poem to me while your friend plays saxophone is not a tasteful way to break up with me. If you're not happy with things, just tell me, and be honest instead of flowery. It's baffling and a little stupid and not very well written and frankly, I think I'd rather get an e-mail than this. You could have met me in a coffee shop, or called, or Jesus, even texted. I'd prefer a text to this! I'm not going to crumble like a pillar of salt if you break it to me in a mature way. You need to take off the kid gloves and start treating me like an adult. Oh god, are those finger puppets?

You're Stalking Me

Hey, you! Listen, do you have a minute? I mean, I figure you're not that busy, just hanging out in my laundry hamper. More on that in a minute. Sooo.... I've sort of been thinking that maybe you'd maybe want to stop sending me pictures of yourself with the heart cut out because I "stole" it. Oh god, I hope you're not offended, please don't be offended! It's just like, I've got a few, and they're great, don't get me wrong, but I'm running out of places to put them all! On a related note, I'm just so busy lately, so I don't think I'm going to have the time to run away with you to the "castle in your mind," as your many many notes written in blood have requested. It's like, AHHH, who has time for a vacation in this economy?? Anyway... I love your enthusiasm, I love your dedication to making this thing work (even if I did break up with you a long time ago), and I ADORE the way you're always following me around trying to smell me, but if this continues I'm going to have to mace you in your fucking insane face until your eyeballs are the size of grapefruits. Stay the fuck away from me! TTYN!

You're Cheating on Me

Hey, I'm not old-fashioned, and I'm certainly not the jealous type. I'm a firm believer that men and women can absolutely be friends without it leading to something illicit. That's why I have literally no problem with you hanging out with a member of the opposite sex. I mean, I'm not from Caveman times! By all means, go forth and have a drink! Lord knows you have to unwind a little bit after a long day, and besides, we have plans together tomorrow. So, your friend is really attractive, and you've admitted that you two "may have had a thing" really briefly at one point before we met. You know what I say to that? So what? I'm secure enough in our undying bond of love that I can sleep peacefully knowing that you two are just friends. Although, I *did* hear you on the phone whispering to meet somewhere late at night, and my friends are saying they saw you two making out at a bar last week. However, you can't always trust secondhand information and overheard conversations.

That being said, can you two please put your clothes on and get the fuck out of my apartment?

You Shit Talk Me to Everyone

Whoa, heh. Hey, you! Haven't seen you in a long time. What's it been, two months? Wow. Time flies when you're dealing with the fallout of a painful breakup, right? It's crazy to think that we'd be at the grocery store at the same time! Are these your friends? Hey I'm—hello? Why won't your friends look at me? Why are they walking away from us and pretending to pick up paper towels. What are you telling people about me? Is this why the mailman won't look me in the eye? Jesus, way to burn a bridge or twenty! You ever hear of a little thing called discretion? Or respect? Or not telling strangers I pissed the bed on New Year's Eve? In the immortal words of Bugs Bunny, "Of course you know, this means war." And by THAT, I mean, I'm telling everyone about your vagina situation. You know what I mean. Gauntlet = thrown.

You're REALLY Not Taking This Well

Look, we both know that this hasn't been working for a while. I think it's time to end this—whoa. Put that lamp down. No seriously, step away from the lamp. What were you going to do? Were you going to throw a lamp at my head? Because I tried to break up with you? That's a really heavy lamp. Seriously, wow. I can't even imagine what would have happened if you threw that lamp at me! Like, first of all it would have probably punctured my skull. What if I died? I mean, seriously, what would you do if you murdered me with a lamp? All because I don't want to eat brunch with you anymore? I mean, we're adults. We're allowed to choose who we date, and I just think we've both been sort of phoning it in—HEY!!!!! HEY! Goddammit, you're lucky I have amazing reflexes. JESUS! By the way, that's YOUR lamp, remember? So, you're out one significant other and one significant lamp. Enjoy that.

You Won't Give Me Back My Stuff

Hey, how's everything? Good, I hope. Listen, I'm going out of town for a week, and I wanted to swing by and pick up some stuff before I go. Is that cool? Oh, you know, a few CDs, that stripey shirt, and I actually think my passport is there too. From the time I lost my license and we were going to that club—none of it? No no, I specifically remember where all of those things are. All of them. I have a photographic memory of the layout of your room and I—no, they're not at my place, I'm here right now and I've already torn it apart. I mostly just need that passport so I can go—oh fuck. Don't—are you really keeping my passport from me so I can't go on vacation? That's fucking insane. You're a sociopath. No, coming on vacation with me is not a compromise; it's kidnapping. Or entrapment. Ugh. I can't believe you've seen me naked. That reminds me. If you don't delete those pictures, I'm going to show everyone THOSE pictures.

I'm Doing Really Well Without You

Wow, what a surprise to see you! What's it been, three months now? Thanks, I have been working out... started doing Pilates a few times a week and just wrapped up a juice fast. Actually, I am doing really, really great. After we split up I got offered that huge promotion I had been gunning for. Yup, the one with the seasonal trips to Costa Rica. And that charity I was starting when we were together finally got funding, so I'm getting some humanitarian award for it! I know, right? It's pretty exciting around these parts. Oh, I'm sorry, how rude of me! This is my new boyfriend, Ryan Gosling. Yes, *the* Ryan Gosling.

EPILOGUE

To borrow some wisdom from a certain red-overall-ed plumber friend of ours, sometimes the princess really is in another castle, and there's nothing you can do about it. You spend a whole level jumping around, breaking bricks with your bare hands and stepping on shells and Goombas, and at the end, your reward is, "look somewhere else." Really? But I just spent an entire level literally jumping through hoops for you, baby! I jumped on a turtle for you, and I love turtles! I went into the sewer for you, crawled through a river of shit and slime, and in the end, all I have are a few gold coins and the knowledge that I completed something? Are you kidding me? Unfortunately not, because sometimes there is no reward. You'll just have to settle for some good old-fashioned life experience to make you stronger and more seasoned for the next date, or level, as it were.

Sometimes it takes the courage to count your losses and hit reset and try again. And again and again. Until these moves and codes have become such second nature that, almost effortlessly, Bowser goes down without a fight. And then eventually, in a perfect world, you'll beat the game. Mario gets Peach, Link gets Zelda, and that Tetris piece in the shape on an L gets the perfect square. Everyone wins. But you'll never get there if you don't keep playing.

So maybe that's the moral of this whole thing: hang in there, kittens. We have all these dealbreakers because we're picky, and we're picky because we want to believe that the perfect person is out there, waiting to knock down our door and present themselves to us, perfect smile and all (but not before rebuilding our door). It's this hope that keeps us going, and this secret cockiness that keeps us from settling on someone who's okay but not a perfect match.

It's a crap shoot, a game of trial and error, a coin toss. But it's also fun. We forget how great it can be when someone great comes along and genuinely excites and surprises us. Breakups harden us, bad blind dates repel us, and harmless flirting annoys us. Sometimes you just need to have a sense of humor and reset your internal clock.

You might be single for now, you might hate everything and everyone around you, and you might turn to snarky books that validate your terrible feelings, but no one ever lost any street cred by having hope. That's the kind of shit that keeps us alive! So go out there and knock 'em dead. However, if the results are still nightmarish glimpses into your own private dating hell, don't be surprised, and don't blame us when you find yourself waking up next to a swamp creature from the murky depths of last call. We warned you.

Acknowledgments

The Upright Citizens Brigade Theatre, the chain gang, all of our friends and family, the cupcake brains on Tumblr, Joe Mande, Tae Won Yu, Hannah Gordon at Foundry Media, everyone at Running Press, coffee shops with free wifi, and fine purveyors of pizza everywhere. Thank you most of all to our parents for being so (almost irresponsibly) supportive. We're sorry this book has so many swear words.

About the Authors

Dave Horwitz and Marisa Pinson met while performing Improv and Sketch comedy at the Upright Citizens Brigade Theater in Los Angeles. Together they started the blog Dealbreaker, where they could vent their frustrations about their ill-fated dating lives. Visit their blog at http://dealbreaker.tumblr.com